What Leaders Are Saying About "Grace Immersion"

"Anyone who reads through *Grace Immersion* is going to come out clean and refreshed, feeling like weights have lifted off them and most of all their heart melted in wondrous gratitude to Jesus. But the impact of this book won't end with the reader. As people grasp the message within, their lives will then contagiously impact those who are around them because of the grace they are immersed in. What an incredibly needed message is within these pages about grace, which can literally turn around someone's entire understanding of what it means to follow Jesus."

Dan Kimball
Pastor, Vintage Faith Church
Santa Cruz, California
Author of *They Like Jesus But Not The Church*

"Every Christian I know is looking for what this book describes… And nobody says it with more depth or more humor than René Schlaepfer. If you find yourself needing grace to start over, to overcome a crippling habit, or to let go of guilt, you have picked up the right book. What's at stake? Everything! Every church has scores of people living under dark clouds of condemnation, guilt and hopeless-ness. Christians and the Christian church are at their best (and most attractive) when and only when they are set free by grace!"

Ray Johnston
Senior Pastor, Bayside Church
Granite Bay, California
President of Developing Effective Leaders

"Grace is one of those church words that we use but don't really understand biblically or live freely… *Grace Immersion* will help you understand grace means 'God helps freely' and learn to live in the freedom God graciously gives His children."

Dr. Gerry Breshears
Chair, Division of Biblical and Theological Studies at Western Seminary
Author (with Mark Driscoll) of *Vintage Jesus; Death By Love;* and *Doctrine: What The Church Should Believe*

"If you find your life is dry and joyless, Grace Immersion will help you find the laughter again. And not just through funny stories. René gets to the delightful heart of God's love for you. God's grace is the theme of the whole Bible, so how do we miss it? You'll rediscover it here in bite-sized daily doses that will change you to the core."

Bill Butterworth
Speaker, and author of *On The Fly Guide to Balancing Work and Life; The Promise of the Second Wind* and *When Life Doesn't Turn Out Like You Planned*

"This book rescues grace from the nice theology pile by demonstrating how it can transform your life."

Dr. M. Craig Barnes
Senior Pastor, Shadyside Presbyterian Church, Pittsburgh
Professor of Leadership and Ministry at Pittsburgh Theological Seminary
Author of *Yearning; An Extravagant Mercy*, and more

"Do you want to plunge into the refreshing ocean of God's grace? This book is a perfect diving board! Use the daily meditations, small group resources, songs, and action challenges to launch you into a new and deeper experience of grace."

Kevin Harney
Pastor, Shoreline Community Church
Monterey, California
Author of *Leadership from the Inside Out*; *Seismic Shifts*; and more than sixty small-group Bible studies

"With his new book *Grace Immersion* René takes an area of life that is difficult to know and makes it knowable. This book will engage you when you read it, and will move you. And if you are privileged to be in a small group experience with this book, it can change you. Grace Immersion is not to be missed."

Bert Decker
Chairman and CEO, Decker Communications
TODAY show commentator
Author of *You've Got to Be Believed to Be Heard*; *Speaking with Bold Assurance* and more

"Home run — again! René Schlaepfer helps us connect our deepest daily needs with God's timeless truth. And he does it with vulnerability, skill, and solid Biblical scholarship. *Grace Immersion* helps us receive God's grace in ways that are surprising, powerful, and joyful."

Dru Scott Decker
Psychologist and motivational speaker
Director of www.HeavenTogether.org
Author of *Stress That Motivates*; *Finding More Time In Your Life* and more

"René's teaching on GRACE will bless you and leave you with a great appreciation of God's unending love. This is a book you will definitely enjoy!"

Doug Goodwin
Chief Operating Officer
Kanakuk Ministries
Branson, Missouri

GRACE
IMMERSION

"Grace Immersion: A 50-day plunge into God's amazing grace"

© 2018 Twin Lakes Church, Inc.

ISBN 978-1-4507-3195-9

Sixth printing

If you would like to reproduce or distribute any part of this publication, please contact us:
Twin Lakes Church, 2701 Cabrillo College Drive, Aptos, CA 95003-3103, or email info@tlc.org

Contents

WEEK 4: THE TENSIONS OF GRACE

WEEK 5: GRACE-INSPIRED CHANGE *Grace in Ephesians*

WEEK 6: RIPPLE EFFECTS OF GRACE

WEEK 7: THE WONDERS OF GRACE

SMALL GROUPS *Discussion Questions*

RESOURCES *Project Ideas, Music Playlist & Print Materials*

GRACE
IMMERSION

Introduction

Grace changed my life.

I was a performance-oriented, guilt-ridden Christian when the whole concept of grace turned my world upside down. I almost couldn't believe that what I was reading in the Bible was really there — and that I was discovering it as a pastor, a guy who should have known it all along!

But more about my story later; what about yours?

Never Enough

Do you have a nagging sense that you are never doing enough for God?

Do you wonder what God really thinks of you?

Is "God" to you mostly a vague feeling of guilt and constant disapproval?

Is there a low voice in the background of your life that's always whispering, "that's not quite good enough" — no matter what you do?

Are you afraid that, at the end of it all, maybe you won't make it to heaven?

I've struggled with many of those same feelings for years, and I'm convinced that the problem is, we forget grace.

Forgotten Grace

C.S. Lewis, the famous author of *The Chronicles of Narnia* books, was also a highly respected professor at Oxford. It's in this capacity he was invited to lecture at a comparative religion conference. During lunch on the first day, visiting scholars were discussing what, if anything, is unique about Christianity.

That's when Lewis walked into the room, a little early for his presentation. He sat down and listened to what by now was a fierce debate. Finally he asked, "What's all this rumpus about?"

Everyone turned in his direction. "We're debating what's unique about Christianity," someone said.

"Oh, that's easy," answered Lewis. "It's grace."

It's true: Grace is the Bible's most amazing concept, as startling and fascinating as any philosophical idea or scientific discovery. The doctrine of grace teaches that God is by nature so generous, and I am by nature so spiritually incapacitated, that every aspect of my salvation is 100% a gift from God — because He loves me. Why is it then that Christians often ignore this unique jewel of our faith to focus on other things? It seems we'll talk about any trendy controversy, current headline, or modern fear more than grace. As J. I. Packer says, for many Christians "amazing grace has become boring grace."

Maybe you even picked up this book reluctantly thinking, "Grace? That's baby Christian stuff. 'Jesus loves me this I know.' I got the grace idea way back when I first believed. Nothing for me to learn here."

Really? In my observation, many Christians have some concept of grace in their heads, but it hasn't really moved to their hearts. They still at times feel condemned by God; they still suspect their performance earns them more of God's love; they only think of grace as what saved them, but now their hard work does the rest.

And this is not just about you.

Lost Churches

Today's church needs to rediscover grace as our primary emphasis. If we don't, we're ceasing to be the church. We're preaching the same mix of "try harder" religion and to-do-list spirituality that the Bible condemns.

Immersive Experience

That's why we've put together this Grace Immersion. This is designed, as you can guess from the title, as an immersive experience. For fifty days you'll read about grace, participate in grace projects, talk about grace with friends, listen to songs about grace — and you will see real change.

You'll find yourself making decisions more easily. Feeling more joyful. Praying with greater ease. Reading the Bible with real interest instead of dry duty. Being gentler and kinder with others.

This is all very personal for me. Grace is changing the way I do everything. This book is about the way I see the world, the way I try to lead my church, the way I see my wife and children: It's all different because of grace.

What's Inside?

In Grace Immersion you'll find:

- **50 days of daily meditations**, most with suggested Bible passages to read and verses to contemplate (I encourage you to read this book with an open Bible! You need to make certain for yourself that the radical concepts in this volume are really scriptural). Here's the pathway for these devotions: I start with the gospels to show how grace is emphasized by Jesus. Then I trace the battles over grace through Acts and Galatians, walk through an explanation of the need for grace in Romans, and finally talk about the implications of grace throughout Scripture. Each daily meditation also has personal application questions and a prayer suggestion to help make the principles personal.

- **Seven small group lessons.** We often grow faster when we grow in groups. You'll spur each other on, and inspire each other as you share your insights and struggles. I encourage you to form a group and grow in grace together!

- **Song playlists.** In the back of this book you'll find many more extras, including song playlist suggestions. Download these (legally of course), and then burn a CD or two to listen to as you drive around — grace songs can be a great part of your Grace Immersion!

- We've also included **Grace Project ideas.** Immersing yourself in grace is not just about *learning* grace, but also about *extending* grace.

- **www.GraceImmersion.com** is our web site, which has tons more extras including two weeks of bonus daily devotions, our blog, and more.

- **Video discussion starters.** The small group lessons in this book are designed to tie into the video podcast discussion starters available for free download on the Grace Immersion website. Each short video goes to a different location to illustrate grace or has an intriguing personal story about grace.

This is going to be revolutionary for you.

I believe that real revival can be ignited — in your own spirit, and also in the church — if we refocus on the most unique, the most important, the most stunning, the most head-spinning idea ever: God's grace! Enjoy!

Why Are You Reading This Book?

Maybe you're just starting out as a Jesus-follower. Maybe you're still exploring. A study of *grace* will introduce you to the amazing, fascinating core concept of the Christian faith.

But what if you've been a Christian for years? Is this too basic? No, the Bible says, *"grow in the grace and knowledge of our Lord and Savior Jesus Christ"* (2 PETER 3:18A). The doctrine of grace isn't just for new believers. It's something we're expected to *grow* in as Christians. But why?

Let me put it this way. In college I had a roommate who was one of the most uncouth people I had ever known. If there were the slightest excuse to make a disgusting bodily noise, he'd make it. He wore clothes right out of his dirty laundry pile. Showered once a week (whether he needed it or not!). Told me he was saving money and "avoiding the narrow definition of acceptable odors foisted upon society by pharmaceutical companies" by never wearing deodorant. I argued, pleaded, even mocked him… to no effect. Then almost overnight he changed. Washed and ironed all his clothes. Smelled great. Spoke with eloquence. The reason? *He fell in love.* Suddenly he was delighted to change because of the influence of his new relationship.

Something like that happens when you grow in grace. Once you understand the depths of God's grace, everything changes, from your manners to your activities — and not because someone nagged you either. Because of your new relationship, you'll be changed by love.

In his excellent book *The Grace Awakening*, Charles Swindoll has a great list, that I abridged and added to here, of the ways a study of the doctrine of grace changes you.

In the next 50 days...

1. **You can expect to gain a greater appreciation of God's gifts to you and others.** You'll find your joy and peace growing because you're noticing God's grace all around you.

2. **You can expect to spend less time and energy critical of other peoples' choices.** When you get a grasp on grace, you become less petty and more tolerant. You'll be surprised how relaxed this makes you — and how much easier conversation about Jesus becomes.

3. **You can expect to take a giant step toward maturity.** You'll learn more effective ways to grow and change. You'll find yourself cultivating authentic faith instead of a superficial religion.

4. **You can expect to better understand how the whole Bible fits together**, each element revealing something new about God's grace.

How do you hope to change during this grace study?

Which items on the list do you most long for?

Ask God to help you grow in your understanding of the depths of His grace to you during this study. Go through the list and ask God to develop each of these results in your life during this study. Pray with real expectation!

5. **You can expect to be freed from dry, performance-based religion.** If you've been plagued by a nagging feeling that God is distant, expect that to diminish or even disappear!

So if you've been looking for more joy in your daily life, more consistent victory over temptation, a sense of greater closeness to God, and healthier relationships with others, a study of grace is the place to start!

In fact, it's the only really *effective* place to start. Most systems of self-improvement, religious or not, amount to my efforts as a roommate to cajole my friend into changing. They just don't work, at least not for long.

What *will* change you… is *love*.

REDISCOVERING GRACE

Grace in the Gospels

"My son," the father said, "you are always with me,
and everything I have is yours."

LUKE 15:31

Really Amazing Grace

Read Luke 15:11–31

Trivia question: Of all the songs ever written in any language, which has been recorded most often, by the most artists? The answer: "Amazing Grace." But do you know the dramatic story behind the song?

In the 1700s John Newton was a captain in the British slave fleet. It was a bloody trade. Twenty percent or more of the captives died on every trip from Africa to the slave markets of Jamaica. And by all accounts, Newton was one of the worst sailors in this horrifying profession. He was so immoral that one former captain refused to ever sail with him on the crew, calling him "a Jonah sure to bring God's curses upon any vessel." And Newton was a staunch opponent of Christianity in any form, denouncing God as a myth.

Then one day his ship was caught in the worst storm of Newton's career. Fearing for his life, he cried out to God. And inexplicably, he became a believer.

His skeptical crew thought it just another phony near-death conversion, but his faith stuck. In fact, he eventually left shipping entirely to become a pastor in Olney, England. It was there, in January 1773, that Newton wrote song lyrics to accompany a sermon he was preaching. He meant to demonstrate to his church how he personally felt as he thanked God for His mercies. He called the song *Faith's Review and Expectation* but it became better known by the first two words of the lyric:

> Amazing grace, how sweet the sound
> That saved a wretch like me,
> I once was lost, but now am found,
> Was blind, but now I see.

That first verse uses words from the story of the Prodigal Son, when the father says, *"For this son of mine was dead and is alive again; he was lost, and is found."* The father lavishes gifts on a son who had done nothing but bring shame to his family. That's what grace is — God's unearned, lavish gift of salvation for us sinners (For a fuller definition of grace, turn to page 125).

Newton never could have imagined that words he intended as autobiographical would find resonance in so many millions of hearts. In recent years I've shed tears of gratitude myself singing that song, thinking of my own lostness and God's grace to me.

But only recently.

Why do you think the song "Amazing Grace" resonates with so many people? Does it resonate with you?

To whom do you relate in the parable of the Prodigal Son?

Imagine God saying to you the words in the father's response (v. 31). How would you feel?

Today tell God honestly how you feel about your relationship with Him: Distant, exhausted, confused, happy, sad, or anything else. Ask God to use this study of grace to bring about a "grace revolution" in your heart and mind.

Because here's the forgotten side of the Prodigal Son story: the *older* brother; the Practical Son. His words to the father are telling: *"Look! All these years I've been slaving for you…"*

Sadly, many joyless Christians see themselves exactly the same way: slaving like a servant instead of celebrating like a son. So they work harder and harder trying to be good, desperate to earn the father's attention and approval, all the while blind to the fact that they already have what they strive so earnestly to gain.

I can tell you that while I relate to the younger brother at times, I spent *most* of my Christian life thinking like the *older* brother. I tried so hard not to disappoint my Heavenly Father. Yet I still lived with an unshakable feeling that I just wasn't doing *enough*. So I tried to pray longer, I tried praying on my knees, I read through the whole Bible several times — all the while looking over my shoulder, in a spiritual sense, wondering if my Father was watching and approving.

It all came to a head when I was a pastor, burned out and bitter, yelling in prayer something very much like "All these years I've been slaving for you and never disobeyed your orders — yet I never get to party!!" How did my story end? I'll tell you more tomorrow.

In the parable, the father tries to correct this older son's thinking: *"My son, you are always with me, and everything I have is yours."* But Jesus leaves us hanging, the story unfinished; we never discover the older brother's response. That's because Christ was telling this story to dry, legalistic religious people — to an audience of older brothers (SEE LUKE 15:1–2). *He is leaving the story unfinished because* **we** *finish it with our response.*

I pray that, if you're one of those veteran Christians for whom "amazing grace has become boring grace," as J.I. Packer puts it, you'll have your eyes opened during the Grace Immersion to your Father's love and the riches He lavishes on you!

Born Again... Again!

Read Galatians 5:1–6

> *It is for freedom that Christ has set us free. Stand firm, then, and do not let yourselves be burdened again by a yoke of slavery.* GALATIANS 5:1

From the time I was a teenager until I was a pastor in South Lake Tahoe, California, I struggled with OCD (Obsessive Compulsive Disorder). That's what Jack Nicholson has in the movie *As Good As It Gets*, or what the character Monk had in the TV show of the same name.

It's funny on-screen. But in real life it's maddening: You might be absolutely driven to switch the car radio on and off exactly 50 times, or to touch the right and left sides of your face a certain number of times to "even yourself out." Something tells you that if you fail, bad things will happen. Psychologists call it "ritualistic" behavior.

Finally I was able to break the grip of the OCD — but in many ways it just transferred to my spiritual life. I look back now and call it *spiritual* OCD: my idea that I had to be perfect to please God.

And how did I define perfection? I would decide I had to pray a certain number of minutes every day, and I would — to the minute. Or I had to read a certain number of verses, and I would — precisely.

In fact *precision* became an obsession: I would even pray over my clothes each morning to seek God's guidance on the *precise* things I was to wear. That's how I attempted to find the perfection I believed God wanted me to achieve — after all, doesn't the Bible say to *"be holy as God is holy"*? It all led to a severe case of the "older brother syndrome" I talked about yesterday.

Some of you are thinking, "Ohhh-kayyyy… that's weird." But some of you relate. Your own perfectionistic spirituality has drained you instead of refreshed you. Like other perfectionists, you don't see any numbers between one and ten; you're either giving it all you've got, or you're giving up. You're either working hard at being a great Christian, or you've stopped trying at all, and maybe you even resent the Christian life. The term "ritualistic behavior" describes your Christian life a lot better than "relationship."

I've been there! One writer calls it the Christian "manic-depressive" cycle: laboring feverishly for God or, alternately, discouraged you're such a failure; or experiencing both at the same time!

Of course all of this got exhausting. I was totally dry spiritually, and yet I was a pastor, which just made me feel all the more guilty!

How have you ever lapsed into perfectionism, or legalism — attempting to be perfect and perform religious duties to please God? What happened?

Then one day my whole life changed. I was teaching a Bible study in the book of Galatians. And I read today's verses. And they went off like dynamite in my head. It was like someone suddenly set me free from heavy chains and let me soar. I finally, finally got it — that the Christian life is all about grace!

Grace is used in the Bible to describe God's amazing generosity to the undeserving. Suddenly I saw this thread everywhere. I was particularly intrigued with the grace theme throughout the Gospels. Jesus is described as being so *"full of grace"* (JOHN 1:14) that *"from the fullness of His grace we have all received one blessing after another"* (JOHN 1:16). John summarizes Jesus' ministry this way: *"For the law was given through Moses; grace and truth came through Jesus Christ"* (JOHN 1:17) Grace was all over the place, the major theme of Christ's ministry, the subject of so many parables — like this one:

How easy or difficult is it for you to accept that the Christian life is lived entirely by God's grace?

To some who were confident of their own righteousness, Jesus told this parable:

> *"Two men went up to the temple to pray, one a Pharisee and the other a tax collector. The Pharisee stood up and prayed about himself, 'God, I thank you that I am not like other men — robbers, evil-doers, adulterers — or even like this tax collector. I fast twice a week and give a tenth of all I get.' But the tax collector stood at a distance. He would not even look up to heaven, but beat his breast and said, 'God, have mercy on me, a sinner.' I tell you that this man, rather than the other, went home justified before God."* LUKE 18:10–14A

Pray the prayer of the second guy. Ask God to set you free from performance-oriented religion in the next 50 days! Thank Him for His amazing grace!

His point? Be like the second guy. The first one, the Pharisee, tried to justify himself with his spiritual résumé. But Jesus says the *only one who went home justified* was the one who *knew he had nothing to offer.* God doesn't want me to pretend to be perfect like the Pharisee; He wants me to realize my need for His grace, like the second man.

Seeing grace like this totally rocked my world, zoomed me into a new place. I told my wife, "It's like I've been seeing the world in black-and-white and now it's in color; like I'm born again… *again!*" I'd been a sad perfectionist but now was on my way to becoming a joy-filled believer. But my biggest surprises were yet to come.

It's Just Impossible

Read Matthew 19:16–26

Jesus looked at them and said, "With man this is impossible, but with God all things are possible." MATTHEW 19:26

Yesterday I described myself as a recovering spiritual perfectionist. At the time I thought I was alone, but, like any recovering addict, I soon started meeting a lot of people just like me, people who were performance-oriented, guilt-haunted, and driven by a need to be sure they were pleasing God — yet also exhausted by their efforts.

In fact, I met some in the pages of the Bible, especially in the Gospels as they encountered Christ. Here's the story of one of them.

One day a very rich young man comes up to Jesus — and his question and his attitude remind me so much of my old performance-oriented self. He essentially asks, "What do I need to do to get an *A-plus* from God, to win a golden ticket to heaven?"

I think Jesus is testing him when He says, "Well, keep every single commandment." The man betrays his to-do list mentality as he responds, "Which ones?" Jesus names six commandments — and the man says, "Done!" I honestly do not know how Jesus doesn't burst out laughing here. But He sees into the man's proud soul and says, "Then sell all you own and follow me."

Now the man is going through a major conflict. Think about it: He probably *has* all his stuff precisely because he's so driven. He wants to earn *more* stuff, *more* rewards, not *give away* stuff. Even his *spirituality* seems to be part of his pursuit of trophies. Jesus' words do not compute, so the man walks away.

Then Jesus says something a lot of people miss. The stunned disciples question him, "Who then can be saved?" Jesus then says, *"With man this is…"* What? *"…Impossible."*

As Max Lucado points out in his book *The Applause of Heaven*:

> He doesn't say unlikely. He doesn't even say it will be tough. He says it is impossible. No chance. No way. Impossible. It's impossible to swim the Pacific. It's impossible to go to the moon on the tail of a kite. And unless somebody does something, you don't stand a chance of going to heaven. All your life you've been rewarded according to your performance. That's why the rich young ruler thought heaven was only a payment away. Then Jesus says you don't need a system, but a Savior. You don't need a résumé; you need a Redeemer.

How do you relate to the rich young man's driven personality?

Don't miss it. You cannot save yourself. Not through the right rules. Not through the right ritual. Not through the right religion. It is *impossible* for human beings to save themselves.

But… with God, all things are possible! With God, the prodigal, the prostitute and the priest are all brought into the fold because of His love — not because of what they have earned. That's grace!

How can this become an obstacle to understanding grace?

For a deeper look at grace, see the definition on page 125 and the chart on page 126. In the first group discussion guide, I explore some of the nuances of this fascinating concept. Reading those definitions will help you understand and enjoy the rest of this week's meditations!

Why do people want to cling to their performance-driven motivations? What do you think they are afraid might happen if they let go and simply receive God's grace?

Ask God to help you stop being a performance-driven person when it comes to your faith. Ask Him to help you relax in His grace.

Babies Don't Try To Be Born

Read John 3:1–17

> *In reply Jesus declared, "I tell you the truth, no one can see the kingdom of God*
> *unless he is born again."* JOHN 3:3

Although the word "grace" isn't used very often in the Gospels, the concept is everywhere. Jesus teaches grace constantly. The author of the Gospel of John explains Christ's ministry with the phrase, "the law came through Moses; grace and truth came through Jesus Christ." Most famously, Jesus teaches grace to Nicodemus in John 3.

The top religious scholar in the land, Nicodemus was impressed enough by Jesus to ask for a secret night meeting so he could get to know this new and exciting young teacher. Jesus gets straight to the point: *"You must be born again"* (v. 7).

I want you to realize to whom Jesus was talking.

The Bible says Nicodemus was a *Pharisee*. They were the religious elite. There were never more than 6,000 of them at a time in Israel. Each of them had taken a solemn vow before God and three witnesses to devote their entire life, every moment of every day, to keeping the commandments. They wrote down extra regulations in their rule book, which came to be called the Mishnah, to make sure each commandment was kept, and kept perfectly — for example, just one of the commandments, the one about keeping the Sabbath holy, eventually had *24 chapters* devoted to it in the Mishnah. If there were gold medals in willpower and in religious knowledge, these guys would win every time.

Nicodemus was also a member of the *Sanhedrin*. This was a select group of 70 religious men who ran all the religious affairs of Israel and had moral authority over every Jewish person in the world.

Not only that, but Jesus refers to him in John 3:10 as *the* Teacher of Israel. So Nicodemus apparently had a unique authority in the eyes of the people.

And yet Jesus tells this socially elite, morally upright, super-smart man that even he must be born again.

"Born again." It's one of those overly familiar phrases. But what's it mean?

Well, when you were born did you develop yourself through conscious effort? Did you make your own little feet? "I need ten toes now! Urrrrgh!!" Pop, pop, pop, out came the toes. No. You just grew. I think it's Max Lucado who asks: "How active were you in your birth? Did you shove

Summarize what Jesus meant by "born again" (try to use as little religious language as possible):

yourself out? Were you in radio communication with your doctor: 'Roger, Doc, we are good to GO!'"

No. Someone else did the work. Someone else felt the pain. Someone else made the effort.

Same when you're born spiritually. It's not about your effort. It's about you resting in God's effort on your behalf, knowing *"whoever believes in Him shall not perish but have eternal life."*

What does being "born again" have to do with grace?

Dr. Martin Luther King, Jr.'s daughter Bernice is a pastor, and she puts it this way:

> It makes no difference how much education, money, prestige, power, or pleasure you acquire; if the time and invitation are right, you *will* indulge your nature. That's why you have to be born again; because only when you are born again do you have the *new* nature of God planted in your heart.

If you want to do further study, look up these verses that also talk about being born again: John 1:12–13; James 1:17–18; 1 Peter 1:3; 1 Peter 1:23. What can you learn about the new birth from these verses?

I had to admit that, like Nicodemus, I'd been setting up rules and boundaries to try to earn my salvation. And despite my initial joy, the *practice* of resting in grace still took a long time for me to really understand, as you'll see tomorrow.

Ask God how you can apply this story to your life. Have you been born again?

Stressed, or At Rest?

Read Luke 10:38-42

> *"Martha, Martha," the Lord answered, "you are worried and upset about many things, but only one thing is needed. Mary has chosen what is better, and it will not be taken away from her."* LUKE 10:41-42

I used to dislike today's Bible reading! It confused me. It even made me mad at Jesus. Seems like Mary's a slacker and Martha's… well, Martha's like me! So naturally I just kind of sidestepped this story and put it in the category of weird things Jesus said that no one can possibly understand.

It was only after I understood the doctrine of grace better that I saw in this episode a lesson for life. The lesson? As author Steve McVey says, "Being preoccupied with serving Christ more than with Jesus Himself is a subtle threat to every Christian."

Before you put this in the "I'll think about it later" category, let's do some detective work. When Jesus came to visit Mary and Martha in their home at Bethany, Mary sat down at the feet of Jesus and listened intently to everything He said and watched everything He did. She was focused on Jesus. "But," Luke says, "Martha was distracted with much serving." What? Hit pause for a minute. Luke reports Martha was "distracted." Distracted from what? *From Jesus!* What was it that made her distracted? *Serving Jesus!* See how this story can mess with the head of someone as performance driven as I can be?

So she complains to Jesus about her sister not doing enough work. And does He say, "Martha, Martha, what you are doing is very good, and what Mary is doing is good too. My followers should be a healthy combination of the both of you"? Uh, no, that is not what He says. What He *actually* says is, "*Martha, Martha you are worried and upset about many things, but only one thing is needed.*" How many things? One.

Now before you jump to the conclusion that Jesus doesn't want people to cook and clean, let me ask you this: If He had asked Mary for a drink, do you think she would have sprung to her feet and helped Him out? Of course! But she started with — and stayed with — a restful focus on Christ. It's when we leap into action for Christ without focusing on Jesus and remembering His love for us — without asking Him if He even needs or wants our busyness — that we drift into Martha-ism. Remember that movie *Fatal Attraction*? You could call this syndrome "Fatal Distraction" — distraction from our first love.

To say I can relate to Martha is the understatement of the century.

In what way do you relate to Martha?

In your own words, describe the "one thing" that Jesus says is needed.

Spend some time in prayer today at the feet of Jesus, just gazing at Him, in a spiritual sense. If you're not sure how to do this, start by imagining Him present with you (He really is present, you know!) and then just say thanks. See what happens next.

After the *intellectual* and *emotional* breakthrough I already described, it still took a while for the idea of grace to influence my life at a *practical* level, especially (and ironically) my life as a pastor.

One evening after yet another day at church "being distracted by many things" I came home, fell onto the couch, and thought I was having a stroke. My wife rushed me to the hospital where we discovered that I was having an anxiety attack — the first of several.

The doctor (who, I found out later, attended our church) asked me if I was resting.

I laughed.

He asked if I was getting sleep, exercise, eating a healthy diet, spending time in meditation.

I said I was just too busy.

He prescribed medication *and* a thorough reorientation of my thought process. I began to read Bible verses every day that reminded me of God's sufficiency.

You can find some of those verses, along with other favorites, on page 161 at the back of this book. I encourage you to read them frequently during this Grace Immersion!

I'm still in the process of renewing my mind, but I learned on that day that if I do not focus on that one thing, Jesus Himself, I am very vulnerable to burnout and bitterness. I am much happier, even while busy, if I am focused on *Jesus* and His grace to me.

Religious Grace-Robbers

Read Matthew 23:1–13

Famous author Ernest Hemingway prided himself on living life with no moral code. But few people know he was raised in a conservative Christian family. His grandfather? A friend of the legendary evangelist Dwight L. Moody. His parents? They went to conservative Wheaton College.

Yet when Ernest was just a little boy sitting on his father's lap, his dad would criticize him for saying things "in a wrong way" and immediately spank him and then order him to get on his knees and beg God for forgiveness.

Young Ernest tried so hard to be good. One writer says, "Trouble was, Ernest could never be sure he had been good. He might have done something bad and not known it was bad. It was so hard to obey every rule, so hard to please his mother, his father, his teachers, his minister…"

He sure tried, though. One time Ernest read every word of the King James Bible to win a prize. As a young man he was his church youth group's Program Chairman and then its Treasurer. Worked so hard. Tried so diligently.

Then his father committed suicide. Ernest began writing to ease the pain, but his mother said she was very disappointed in him for "not serving the Lord." One year on his birthday, she sent him as a gift the gun his father had used to kill himself. In the card she wrote again about how disappointed she was in her son.

Is it any wonder Hemingway eventually rebelled, rewriting the Lord's Prayer as "Our nada who art in nada, nada be thy name"? Is it any wonder he said, "My soul feels as empty as a vacuum tube"? Any wonder that he became known for his womanizing, drinking ways, trying to find freedom from a stifling upbringing by going as far as he could in the other direction? Is it any wonder he found no freedom there either and ended his life in the same way his father had?

Bad religion can kill people.

How do you think Jesus feels about the kind of religion Hemingway was exposed to? In today's passage, Jesus skewers the religious leaders of His day for a performance-oriented religion that He says can actually shut the kingdom of heaven in men's faces.

Maybe you also experienced what author David Seamands calls "dysgrace" from parents or religious authorities. That's his term for any system or relationship that essentially teaches the opposite of grace. It's so difficult to unlearn these patterns. But it is possible!

In Mark 10:42, Luke 22:25, and 1 Peter 5:1–3 church leaders are told not to "lord it over" people under their care. What does it mean for a Christian leader to "lord it over" someone? How does this relate to grace?

How can a faith meant to set people free become a means of oppression?

Is your faith making you feel weary and burdened, or is it light and easy?

Pray that you will be an example of someone leading by grace, not law. Pray for the leaders in your church — that they will grow in their skill at leading people into a relationship with God and true holiness through grace.

In my observation, churches today don't usually express "dysgrace" in *classic* legalism (as in, you have to keep the Hebrew law), but in a form of legalism you could call *moralism*. Moralistic leaders provide a cut-and-dried list of what is right and what is wrong, and then define the goal of Christianity as keeping those rules.

Because these leaders see themselves as helping people live up to certain *standards*, their job becomes mainly about explaining the rules, training people how to keep rules, teaching people how to interpret Scripture to find rules, and finding out whether or not people are keeping the rules. Consequently they are able to produce only two things: rule-keepers or rule-breakers. Either way, their followers' souls are empty as vacuum tubes.

Jesus talked *a lot* about the danger of such law-oriented leadership.

He pointed out how in such systems that even Bible study, instead of being a way to get to know God better, becomes an end in itself — or a search for more rules:

> *"You diligently study the Scriptures because you think that by them you possess eternal life. These are the Scriptures that testify about me, yet you refuse to come to me to have life."* JOHN 5:39–40

Instead of helping people begin a relationship with God, He said these leaders were oppressing people with pressure to perform. *"They tie up heavy loads and put them on men's shoulders, but they themselves are not willing to lift a finger to move them"* (MATTHEW 23:4).

That's why Christ's offer of grace was so appealing:

> *"Come to me, all you who are weary and burdened, and I will give you rest. Take my yoke upon you and learn from me, for I am gentle and humble in heart, and you will find rest for your souls. For my yoke is easy and my burden is light."* MATTHEW 11:28–30

If *easy, light,* and *rest* are not words you associate with your faith, then you may be under the heavy yoke of religion instead of the yoke of Christ.

Colorful or Colorless Christians?

Read Matthew 23:15–28

A few years ago, our church gave away our pews to a Russian congregation. They rented a flatbed truck and came to pick them up — and we have a lot of pews, so loading and transporting them was a two-day job. I really loved listening to these guys speak in their super-thick accents and (for some reason) ultra-loud voices, so I hung around and kept talking to them, eventually daring to ask them to read things I wrote down, like, "We must get that moose, Natasha!" and "Captain Kirk, it was Khan!" which they did with great volume and gusto. Amusing to me, although I'm pretty sure they had no idea what they were talking about.

Then toward the end of the day, I asked them, "Where are you staying tonight?" And these guys answered (and you have to imagine this in their accent): "Ve are sleeping here in church!" Immediately I thought, "I see that every weekend!" But out loud I said, "Do you need sleeping bags? I can go get some…"

And they said, "NO! We are putting pews together in shape of — what is word? — casket? *Da! CASKET!* And ve are sleeping in *CASKET* made of *PEWS!*"

I said, "But what if you guys get cold? Want some blankets?" And they answered, "*NO!* When ve are getting cold ve are getting up in night and *WORKING HARDER!*" And the other guys chimed in: "*DA!* When getting cold, *WORKING MORE!*"

And as I walked away that night it occurred to me: What a great metaphor for what church can become. It turns from something with life into something dead. Pews into caskets. Then when we feel our souls get cold our solution is: WORK MORE! WORK HARDER! That's where I was coming from for many years. And that's what I see in so many Christians around me.

In today's verses, Jesus continues expressing frustration about the Pharisees who, with their complex system of religion, turn pews into caskets.

In fact, religious legalism is the cultural evil Jesus criticizes more than any other. That's because He sees a faith that should be setting people free, putting them in spiritual chains instead. No wonder Christ's grace-filled message was such a relief.

I think *The Message*'s paraphrase of Jesus' words we saw yesterday in Matthew 11:28–30 captures the way Jesus must have sounded to people in His culture longing for some solution to their cold, worn out feeling (other than "work harder"):

How would you answer Eugene Peterson's questions — how does the "colorless" picture of Christianity get painted on so many imaginations?

Do an honest self-appraisal: Do you reflect grace or legalism to others?

Today tell God where you feel weary and burdened. Tell Him that you take His yoke upon you, the yoke that is easy and light.

Are you tired? Worn out? Burned out on religion? Come to me. Get away with me and you'll recover your life. I'll show you how to take a real rest. Walk with me and work with me — watch how I do it. Learn the unforced rhythms of grace. I won't lay anything heavy or ill-fitting on you. Keep company with me and you'll learn to live freely and lightly. MATTHEW 11:28–30 [THE MESSAGE]

"Freely and lightly." Does that describe your Christian walk? I like what Eugene Peterson says in his book *Traveling Light*:

> The word Christian means different things to different people. To one person it means a stiff, uptight, inflexible way of life, colorless and unbending. To another it means a risky, surprised-filled venture, lived on tiptoe at the edge of expectation. Either of these pictures can be supported with evidence. There are numberless illustrations for either position in congregations all over the world. But if we restrict ourselves to biblical evidence, only the second image can be supported. If we get our information from the biblical material, there is no doubt — I repeat — there is no doubt that the Christian life is a dancing, leaping, daring life!
>
> How then does this other picture get painted in so many imaginations? How does anyone get the life of faith associated with dullness, with inhibition, with stodginess? We might reasonably expect that a group of people who… have been told stories of Jesus setting people free… would be sensitive to any encroachment… but in fact the community of faith, the very place where we are most likely to experience the free life, is also the place where we are in most danger of losing it. (Quoted in Swindoll, p. 82–83)

Sadly, the movement Jesus founded itself became rapidly infected by the same legalism He criticized. After the ascension of Jesus some of the first churches began to resemble the Pharisees more than Christ.

And no one was more qualified to see this than a former Pharisee.

Tomorrow you'll see the surprising developments that led a world champion legalist to become the Apostle of Grace!

FIGHTING FOR GRACE
Grace in Acts and Galatians

Are you so foolish? After beginning with the Spirit,
are you now trying to attain your goal by human effort?

GALATIANS 3:3

Give Me Liberty!

Read Acts 15:1–11

My wife is related to Patrick Henry, one of the founding fathers of the United States. His most famous moment came on March 23, 1775, when he addressed the Virginia Convention at a dramatic crossroads in American history: "If we wish to be free, we must fight!" he said. "I know not what course others may take, but as for me, give me liberty or give me death!"

Sometimes you have to fight for freedom.

Today's verses are thrilling for me because they describe a similar drama swirling around one of the most important decisions in the history of the Christian church — maybe the most important decision of all.

Until this moment disciples of Jesus were considered by most people as a sort of branch of Judaism. Then something surprising happens: People of other religions start to become followers of Jesus in great numbers.

So naturally many of the first generation of Christians insist that these new converts follow the traditional Jewish religious rules, especially those in the Hebrew Scriptures. This includes all the dietary restrictions for kosher food, circumcision of males, rules for appropriate dress, observing holy days, etc., etc.

But Paul (more on him tomorrow) and Barnabas, two upstart Christian teachers who've been finding eager audiences among non-Jews, disagree. They see Jesus not only as a Jewish Messiah, but as the Messiah for the entire world. If this is so, they argue, why would Jesus care if these new non-Jewish believers adopt Jewish religious customs? They point to Christ's own teaching about the dangers of legalism and performance-oriented religion. What matters is not circumcision or diet or dress or holidays, they assert. What matters is *"faith expressing itself through love"* (GALATIANS 5:6B). Jews, Gentiles, slaves, freemen — they are all welcomed in by *grace*, through *faith*.

This debate erupts into a controversy that threatens to blow apart the whole movement. So Paul, Barnabas, and some of the other leaders go to Jerusalem, center of the early church. There they meet with elders including none other than Peter, the well-known disciple of Jesus Himself, and James the half-brother of Jesus.

Imagine the tension as Paul makes his case. Then these icons of the faith stand up… and stun many in Jerusalem by taking Paul's side!

Why would people turn back to religious legalism after being taught grace (like many of Paul's early converts did)? What's the appeal?

Do churches today ever unwittingly "make it difficult" for people turning to faith by putting on them heavy religious burdens? How so?

The decision of Peter and James was a dramatic one, but it didn't happen in a vacuum. What teachings of Jesus — or episodes from their own lives — could have led them to their conclusion that everyone is saved by grace, not works? (Review last week's devotions for clues.)

Ask God to help you stay free from the bondage of legalism. Pray specifically for new believers in your church. Ask God to help them stay devoted in a simple and pure way to Jesus Christ, without unnecessary religious burdens that could steal their joy.

In fact Peter rebukes the religiosity of those scrupulously applying their own traditions to the Gentiles:

> *"Now then, why do you try to test God by putting on the necks of the disciples a yoke that neither we nor our fathers have been able to bear? No! We believe it is through the grace of our Lord Jesus that we are saved, just as they are."* ACTS 15:10–11

And James agrees: *"It is my judgment, therefore, that we should not make it difficult for the Gentiles who are turning to God"* (ACTS 15:19).

This was one of the most important events in the history of the early church because it set the DNA for the faith: Authentic, vintage Christianity was to be about grace, not law; faith, not works.

You can understand why Paul, having fought for this freedom at the Jerusalem council and believing he had achieved victory, was upset when, as he planted new churches, religious legalizers simply followed in his tracks and taught the naive new believers the very theology that was condemned by Peter and James!

That's what's behind the emotion in so many of his letters to these young communities of believers, like the letters to the Galatians and Colossians. Paul cries "Liberty!" in the face of legalism.

We'll be looking at Paul's Patrick Henry-like passion this week!

The Guardian of Grace

Read Galatians 1:3–7

> *I am astonished that you are so quickly deserting the one who called you by the grace of Christ and are turning to a different gospel — which is really no gospel at all. Evidently some people are throwing you into confusion and are trying to pervert the gospel of Christ.* GALATIANS 1:6–7

In the first week of Grace Immersion you saw how Jesus taught against performance-driven religion at every turn. But then yesterday you saw this teaching in danger of being lost almost immediately as the early church drifted back to legalism.

So God raised up a very unusual man to protect this legacy: a Pharisee, of all people, named Saul — a guy who had been absolutely opposed to the Christians until his sudden conversion. His named changed to Paul, this former teacher of religious law became the unlikeliest champion of grace!

In fact you could call Paul the Apostle of Grace. Of the 155 times the New Testament uses the word *grace*, 133 are found in his writings. Grace opens his letters, grace closes his letters, and grace is the point of everything in between. Paul enthusiastically makes one point over and over again in his biblical writings: Grace alone is, was, and always will be the basis of our relationship with God.

So it's like some kind of sad reverse miracle that this constant emphasis on grace is lost on so many people who conclude Christianity means the exact opposite. Ask most people what the Bible teaches and you'll get a variation on the idea, "Do less bad things and more good things, and then you'll please God and go to heaven."

This exact confusion was happening even in the churches Paul helped start.

As he says in today's verses, he is *"astonished"* that the Galatians are *"so quickly deserting"* the grace of Christ and turning to a different gospel. As he adds, it's really *"no gospel at all"* because *gospel* means *good news*, and it's not good news to hear that you have to work your way to heaven!

So what happened to the Galatians? Some teachers came along and taught a doctrine you could label *Christ Plus*: Jesus died for your sins, but now there are a bunch of extra religious hoops for you to jump through. You might be *forgiven* by God's grace, but you continue on from there with your own hard work. This subtle and insidious teaching poisons the minds of many Christians today, just as it did in Paul's day.

*How does an understanding of **grace** lead to **peace?***

In fact, maybe *your* mind is poisoned. Maybe you picked up this book reluctantly, thinking, "Grace? That's baby Christian stuff. 'Jesus loves me' — this I know, already! I got the idea that I'm saved by grace way back when I first believed. Nothing for me to learn here."

I beg to differ. In my observation, many, if not most, of the Christians I know have some concept of grace in their *heads*, but it hasn't really moved to their *hearts*. They still feel condemned at times by God; they still suspect their performance earns them more of God's love; they only think of grace as what saved them, but now their hard work does the rest. In fact, for them the gospel has been *perverted* into something that really is not *gospel* at all.

Do you think some of the lack of peace you may be experiencing is tied to a lack of understanding about grace?

It's interesting that Paul opens most of his letters with the phrase *"grace and peace to you."* When you *get* grace, really understand it, you also experience *peace*, real peace, deep down in your soul. So how's *your* peace level?

As you continue this Grace Immersion with a look at how Paul clarifies and champions the concept of grace, I know you'll find your peace level growing!

Ask God to help you see the full, dynamic, outrageous truth of the gospel of grace during this Grace Immersion. Ask God to deliver you from a watered-down grace or grace mixed with human messages.

What Kind of Commitment?

Read Galatians 3:1–10

> *Are you so foolish? After beginning with the Spirit, are you now trying to attain your goal by human effort?* GALATIANS 3:3

Growing up in the San Francisco Bay Area I often heard the Oakland Raiders' team motto, "Commitment To Excellence."

That could have been my personal motto as a Christian! I was *committed* to do better. And when I inevitably failed, I would *recommit* my life to trying harder for Jesus. That commit-fail-recommit cycle was my lifelong pattern. And it wasn't working.

I still believe God wants people to commit their lives to Him. *But there's a lot of confusion about the definition of commitment.*

In English, "commitment" has two definitions that are almost opposites. "Commitment" can mean trying harder (as in the Raiders' motto) or it can mean the exact opposite (as in the Raiders' play on the field! Just kidding!).

Here's an example of the *second* kind of commitment: When my wife *committed* herself to the care of the doctor before her surgery (gall bladder surgery if you must know, and she's fine, thank God!), her commitment meant that she *surrendered control* to the surgeon. She *yielded.* She *trusted* the doctor entirely. She certainly wasn't on the operating room table saying, "I'm trying real hard to give him my gall bladder! Ooomph!" No — she wasn't even awake!

It's that *second* kind of commitment that God wants me to make to Him.

When I committed my life to Jesus Christ, I surrendered my will entirely to His care. Having proven that my self-efforts were incapable of producing life-saving change, I gave up to God and had a spiritual rebirth. Most Christians understand that part. But here's where we go wrong: the key to *growing* my character is to *remain committed*, in the *second* sense of the word, to His care.

As Paul points out in today's verse, the Galatians had slipped from the second definition of commitment back to the first. Having started their Christian lives by grace, they were now trying to get the rest of the way to Christ-like character through mere human effort, just as they had been living — without success — before they became Christians.

I really get that. For many years my faith, which I *called* Christianity, was really *Churchianity:* just garden-variety "try harder" religion based on rules and human effort. It had a thin veneer

Which definition of "commitment" is dominant in your life?

Why is it so easy for Christians to slip from the second definition of "commitment"(yielding) back to the first (trying hard)?

Today, yield your life to God, maybe for the first time or as a re-surrender. Give to Him the areas of worry or compulsion, or addiction you are struggling with today.

of Christian theology. I had trusted in Christ to save me from sin. But after that, I lived like I was on my own again.

Instead of a whole new way of thinking and living, I had just made a short detour from the standard religious road of self-effort. I did "accept Jesus." Then I was right back at it, doing just what I had always done: trying harder to do more. *My efforts were really indistinguishable from any devout performer in any other religious system.*

But real Christianity is something else: *"We have been released from the law so that we serve in the new way of the Spirit, and not in the old way of the written code"* (ROMANS 7:6).

Notice how Paul says we still serve, but we serve in the *new way* of the Spirit, and not the *old way* of the written code. My entire motivation for obedience has changed from rule-keeping to a more mature desire to grow closer to the God who lavishes His love on me! More on that tomorrow!

Your Father's Voice

Read Galatians 4:1–7; 5:1–4

> A four-year old girl was overheard whispering into her newborn baby brother's ear.
>
> "Baby," she whispers, "tell me what God sounds like. I am starting to forget."
>
> (Quoted in Robert Bensen, *Between the Dream and the Coming True*, p. 55)

When we're newborn baby Christians we love to listen to our Heavenly Father's voice as He sings us grace-songs. But as we grow older in our faith we sometimes forget what He really sounds like. I know I did.

As a child I was delighted to accept God's free gift of salvation, because, like most little kids, there really wasn't a lot I could do for myself — in any way. I needed a boost to reach the water fountain, so I sure wasn't going to think twice when told I needed a boost to reach heaven. So how did I spiral down from there to the point that my religiosity was crippling my spirit?

There were many contributing factors, among them the OCD I already mentioned. But another was even more insidious: I really enjoyed achieving *excellence*. I was an honor student who liked working hard, and I enjoyed the rewards of hard work. Slowly, without even realizing it, I allowed that to subtly change the emphasis of my faith from grace to works. I figured that since God was perfect, He appreciated excellence, and the more excellent I was, the more He'd appreciate me. Specifically, if I were excellent at keeping religious rules (even those imposed by human leaders) and religious restrictions (such as resting on the Sabbath), I would really be loved! I'd heard lots of messages condemning "lukewarm faith" so I determined I would burn hot for God — as evidenced by my hard work for Him (Except for on the Sabbath! When I would *rest* hard for Him!).

But in today's passage, Paul says this kind of thinking is *"slavery."* He even says you can become *"alienated from Christ"* by your hard religious work! That was me: Rather than enjoying my Father, I began to imagine Him as a hard-to-please employer. I thought I heard mostly condemnation from Him; I was never really at peace; I felt like I ought to do more, could do more, should do more… And instead of asking whether I was in theological error, I began to resent Him just like an under-appreciated employee! I even would go "off the reservation" into my own personal Mardi Gras of indulgence once in a while because my whole life felt like one long Lenten fast. Then I'd crawl back feeling guiltier than ever.

But listen to the real voice of God again: *"…you are no longer a slave, but a son; and since you are a son, God has made you also an heir."* (GALATIANS 4:7) I still remember how, when I read that passage the night of my "re-rebirth," I wept. *No longer a slave, but a son!* There's a big difference:

Do you tend to think of yourself as God's slave, God's child, or some combination?

Read Galatians 4:5–7 out loud, but personalize it, saying your name at each pronoun.

Today, pray the prayer from Dr. Seamands' book: "Father, dear Father, I am your child, and I'm going to live and feel like one!"

A slave is *always worried* he'll displease his master; a child is *secure* in the love of his family.

My friend Mike Yaconelli once led a one-day church retreat where attenders read different Scriptures and wrote down what they thought God might say to them today. When they were asked to read their compositions aloud, the adults found it difficult, so Janie, a 17-year-old high school girl, volunteered to read hers first. Here is her dialogue with God as recorded in Mike's book *Dangerous Wonder*, starting with her voice, followed by what she imagines God would say, based on Scripture:

> i feel awkward
> because it's been so long since i've been near you
>> i've missed you too;
>> i think about you every day.
> But i've messed up;
> i've done a lot of things that i regret
>> it's okay, child;
>> i forgive you.
> i don't understand
> i turn away, i ignore you…
>> i'm still here
>> right beside you.
> i try to live without you
> even though i know deep inside that you're still a part of me
>> you don't have to make yourself lovable;
>> i love you how you are.
> even after everything i've done, and after everything that has happened;
> would it offend you if i called you bizarre?
>> i am bizarre;
>> more so than you'll ever know.
> this may seem strange but
> could i please ask you to hold me, for a little while?
>> my child, i've been waiting for you
>> with outstretched arms.

Mike says that after Janie read her dialogue there wasn't a dry eye in the place, and all the adults said, "I'm not reading mine."

Christianity really isn't so complicated. You can learn once again to hear the grace-filled whisper of God.

Kudzu Control!

Read Galatians 5:5–9

> *A little yeast works through the whole batch of dough.* GALATIANS 5:9

If you've ever driven along a road in the Southern United States, you've seen kudzu vine climbing all over entire forests.

This invasive plant was first introduced to the U.S. in an exhibit at the Philadelphia Centennial Exposition in 1876. Gardeners who grew kudzu as ground cover soon discovered to their chagrin that climate conditions in the South are ideal for it to grow completely out of control. The U.S. now loses over half a billion dollars a year in lost crop and control costs, thanks to kudzu! It's tough to control because pulling down the vines does nothing to kill the plant; you have to locate and sever the "root crown" from the rest of the vine, and this root crown is often hidden.

Well, performance-orientation is the kudzu vine of Christianity.

It's a non-native intruder that starts small but soon completely takes over, smothering every part of the Christian life: daily devotions that started as a time of refreshment become dry daily duty; church attendance becomes less about celebrating God's lavish love than about learning how to be better people; even parenting, which should be inspired by God the Father's grace toward us, becomes performance-driven and guilt-inducing. It's the little yeast that works through the whole batch of dough, completely changing it.

As the author to the Hebrews warns, *"See to it that no one misses the grace of God and that no bitter root grows up to cause trouble and defile many"* (HEBREWS 12:15).

My friend Ray Johnston points out three results of "missing grace":

- **Perfectionism** (A lack of grace turned *inward*)

- **Judgmentalism** (A lack of grace turned *outward*)

- **Legalism** (A lack of grace turned *upward*)

In each case, they're "bitter roots." I get bitter toward myself, or toward others, or toward God.

And like kudzu, performance-orientation is tough to kill. You have to aim for the "root crown": the idea that I can, in any way, earn part of my salvation or earn more of God's love. Once I allow this as a possibility, the climate is right for performance-orientation to take over everything.

Which of the three results of missing grace have you struggled with most?

How does missing the grace of God lead to "bitter" roots?

Ask God to help you see if you are missing the grace of God in some area of your life now, using the three results of missing grace as a template: Are you a perfectionist, judgmental, or legalistic? Ask God to show you if you have a "bitter root." Ask Him to help you root it out.

I protect against that idea by refreshing myself repeatedly with the truth of grace: There is nothing I can do to make God love me more, and there is nothing I can do to make God love me less. He promises that He loves me and saves me with His infinite, unconditional, all-sufficient grace!

One of the most tragic errors that churches often make is to over-emphasize the work that believers should be doing for God. That is fertile ground for the vine of performance-orientation. As Chuck Smith puts it in his book *Why Grace Changes Everything*:

> How many times have you heard heavy, condemning sermons that tell you, "You ought to be praying more! You ought to be giving more! You ought to be witnessing more, or serving God on some committee more!" How often do you go to church looking for encouragement only to hear about your failure and how disappointed God must be in you?
>
> The last thing I need is for someone to lay a heavy burden on me about my failures. I know I ought to be doing more. No one needs to tell me I don't read my Bible enough or pray enough. All I get from such messages is a huge guilt complex. My frustration increases because I really want to love God more, to pray more, to have a deeper fellowship with Him. When we place our emphasis on areas of failure, we end up creating defeated, discouraged Christians who give up and drop out of the race.

Look at the New Testament letters and you will see a totally different emphasis. Again and again, they lay a foundation not of what *we* ought to be doing for *God*, but what *God* has already done for *us!*

But you may be wondering, "If it's not about my *performance*, then how does grace-oriented Christianity change my life? If I am saved by grace, why does being a Christian make me so tired? What am I doing wrong? Turn the page.

Are You Rowing or Sailing?

Read Galatians 5:13–25

> *Walk by the Spirit, and you will not carry out the desire of the flesh.*
> GALATIANS 5:16 [NASB]

I love walking out to the lighthouse at the Santa Cruz harbor at sunset. Graceful sailboats glide through the narrow inlet. Rowers and kayakers paddle hard past the rocks on the way home.

Now, I know some people love rowboats, but I can tell you they're a lot slower than sailboats and, by the looks on the faces of the rowers, a lot more work!

I used to live like a rowboat Christian.

I saw daily Bible reading, prayer, witnessing, etc., all as strokes of the oar, good deeds that might get me to the destination — God's blessing — some day! But before long, my exertions wiped me out and I was rowing in circles.

And to keep from total despair I was redefining progress: It became all about the paddling. Putting the oars in the water became my focus. I forgot about the destination. Bible reading, Scripture memory, quiet time became my goals. Spiritual growth came to be about the means, not the end.

But God intends you to make progress like a sailboat, not a rowboat.

The disciplines of the spiritual life are like the sails of the boat: Bible reading, prayer, and so on are *sails* meant to catch the breeze and help you move forward with the wind. They help you see, feel, and appreciate God's gracious love. And *that's* what moves you forward. The way you set your sails helps you catch the wind, but it's the wind that propels you — the *wind* is the energy source, not *you*. It's exhilarating!

When I began awakening to the truth of grace, I felt like I was unfurling my sails, starting to zip along with the breeze of the Spirit, making progress in my character growth like never before! I was still doing spiritual "disciplines", but there began to be a difference in the effect they had on my life. Incrementally, the more I read the Bible, sang worship songs, shared my faith, prayed, etc., the more *revitalized* I felt — instead of feeling *drained*, as these exact same activities had made me feel before.

The difference? I realized these disciplines were not earning me anything — they were just *sails*, put up to help me sense the surge of grace that had always been there, but that I had ignored while I was rowing my way around!

In what way do you relate to the rowing vs. sailing metaphor?

Has your spiritual life been characterized more by rowing or sailing?

Today in prayer put up your sails, so to speak, and thank God for His love and grace to you. Prayer for specific people you know, that they may understand God's grace through Christ for them.

And I realized they were the *means* to the *end*. The goal was a Christ-like spirit: "*Love, joy, peace, patience, kindness, goodness, faithfulness, gentleness and self-control*" (GALATIANS 5:22–23).

Ironically, when I am in my "rowing" state of mind, I often have *less* fruit of the Spirit; the hard work makes me crabby and cramped. I display what Paul calls in today's passage *"desire of the flesh"*: certainly the jealousy, selfish ambition, envy, and spirit of discord in my life seems to be intensified by my grunt work (GALATIANS 5:20–21). I think it's because I feel almost as if I am in competition with the other rowers.

The thrill of living by grace, on the other hand, develops Christ-like attributes more quickly than "rowing" ever does!

I encourage you to put up your sails! And if that analogy doesn't work for you, Paul's got another one up his sleeve for tomorrow!

Seeds of Grace

Read Galatians 6:7–18

I remember when I was in fourth grade the teacher had each of us plant a bean seed in a Styrofoam cup filled with soil.

I waited and waited for what seemed like months (probably a week!). I wanted so much to help that little seed grow that I finally dug it up to see how it was doing. I saw the tiniest little root, so I put it back. Next day, I dug it up again to see what was going on. Not much progress. Buried it. Dug it up again later that day to see very little growth. Tugged on the root to help out a little. Buried it again. Repeat hourly.

You can guess how that turned out. I was the only kid in class who couldn't even grow a bean. Why? I was trying too hard to make something happen!

When it comes to your spiritual growth, maybe you need to stop trying so hard. Stop being so introspective, digging up the bean to see what's growing. Instead, plant good seeds, make sure they're watered, and relax a little. In time you'll see the crop. That's what Paul says in today's potentially confusing passage.

Remember, the Galatians had slipped back to legalism after starting their Christian walk by grace. So through this whole letter, Paul shows them how God is all about grace, grace, grace.

Then, toward the very end of the letter, Paul says something that may totally surprise you because it sounds like he's going right back to the old, tired religious formula of "you get what you earn":

> *Do not be deceived: God cannot be mocked. A man reaps what he sows. The one who sows to please his sinful nature, from that nature will reap destruction; the one who sows to please the Spirit, from the Spirit will reap eternal life.* GALATIANS 6:7–8

Uh… this sounds a lot like… *earning salvation* to me. So am I saved by grace, or do I reap what I sow?

Read it in context: In this passage Paul's talking about how you can enjoy the results of God's grace in your life. When you plant *seeds* of grace, you will reap the *fruit* of grace. When you plant *seeds* of destruction, you reap the *fruit* of destruction.

It's *God* who changes you. But you can *cooperate* in one way: repentance. In Greek, the word for repentance literally means to "change my mind" (really, every other "spiritual discipline" is just a form of this one). This works because you always *move toward* whatever you *focus on*. Every

How does the concept of sowing and reaping help you understand how to grow spiritually?

How can you sow seeds of grace in your life, and in others' lives, today?

Ask God to help you plant good seeds of grace in your soul each day.

moment spent gazing in wonder at Christ, every act of grace done in the name of Christ, every prayer spent thanking God for His grace — these are all seeds that will slowly grow as the focus of my mind is changed.

And what kind of a harvest is my goal? Not Bible study or prayer as ends in themselves — those are ways I water the seeds.

What grows from the seed? As we read yesterday: *"…love, joy, peace, patience, kindness, goodness, faithfulness, gentleness and self-control."* (GALATIANS 5:22–23) This is the consequence, the reward, of godly, grace-full living: I am increasingly filled with love and joy and peace and more. *But if what I'm doing is not producing that harvest, then I need to rethink what I'm doing.*

I think this is why some people I know — people who have the most incredible Bible knowledge and the strictest moral code — also come across as the least kind, the least gentle, the least joyful people. They've been focusing *not* on Jesus and those qualities of Christ-likeness as their intended harvest, but on the spiritual disciplines themselves or producing "results" for God.

How does this shift in focus happen? Speaking here from my own experience, you start by constantly checking the bean seeds like I did in fourth grade, wanting so badly to see spiritual growth. And because qualities like joy or kindness are hard (if not impossible) to accurately measure, you start focusing on more *quantifiable* things — like time spent in Bible study or prayer or on mission trips. And so you become more studious or more disciplined, since that's what you're measuring, but not more joyful or kind.

The lesson I learned from years spent living this way? It's much better to relax, plant some seeds, and *let them grow*. And remember to keep looking at the picture on the seed packet: It's a picture of Jesus.

As Joshua Harris comments, "Holiness isn't a mysterious spiritual state that only an elite few can reach. It's more than an emotion, or a resolution, or an event. Holiness is a harvest." It takes time and an easy-going patience that is at odds with a performance-driven Christianity.

WHY GRACE?
Grace in Romans

For all have sinned and
fall short of the glory of God,
and are justified freely by his grace
through the redemption that came
by Christ Jesus.

ROMANS 3:23–24

Bad News First

Read Romans 1:18–20, 3:10–18

"Do you want to hear the good news or the bad news first?"

How do you answer that question? I always want to hear the bad news first. Get it out of the way. Rip the bandage off fast and move on (plus, when you hear the bad news first, the good news sounds even better!).

The Book of Romans begins in a place where all the news seems very, very bad.

After writing several letters (like Galatians) where he put out the fires of legalism with the water of grace, Paul apparently decided to write this letter to the church in Rome to systematically teach them the gospel of grace.

He starts with what sounds like the bad news: God is angry at evil. But Paul tells us God is *right* to be angry at evil. Love is *always* angry at evil.

Don't confuse the wrath of God with the wrath of man. Human anger often comes from a selfish trigger ("I am offended!" "I feel disrespected!") and is often expressed with unpredictable explosions of temper. But God doesn't get angry like that. As Max Lucado says, "God is angry at the evil that ruins His children."

As I write this, BP is still trying to cap an oil gusher far below the surface of the Gulf of Mexico. Crude oil is spewing into the sea following a tragic explosion on a deep-sea drilling rig. Beautiful white beaches and delicate marsh lands are being soiled.

People are right to be angry and upset about this, right to demand justice, right to ask that recompense be made. The disaster already cost precious human lives in the initial explosion and continues to pollute the environment. Cleanup will be expensive. Doesn't all that make you mad — and sad?

Well, I believe when you experience grief and anger over that oil spill you get a glimpse of how God must feel about evil on this planet. He's sad and angry at evil because to Him it's rancid pollution of what He made as a perfect place. It's a sickening tragedy. It must be cleaned up. Cleanup will be costly. And recompense must be paid.

And I hate to tell you this but there's more bad news: In this metaphor, we're all BP.

You and I have all, in many ways large and small, contributed to fouling the environment God meant to be a perfect Eden for humanity. There was an initial explosion when our ancestors first

How would you explain how love and anger could co-exist in God?

rebelled against God, and since then, with hatred, with insults, with selfishness, we've all spewed more oil into the ocean. *"As the Scriptures say, 'No one is righteous — not even one.'"* (ROMANS 3:10 [NLT])

This is your spiritual predicament — and mine.

How is the wrath of God different from the wrath of humans?

You and I need to first understand this bad (but true) news: the enormity of sin, and the very justified wrath of God against it.

Only then can we fully appreciate the beautiful, astounding, undeserved, lavish gift of grace. Grace is the amazing story of the perfect cleanup. The paid debt. The good news that comes next.

How is the problem of human sin like the oil spill?

Thank God for His mercy even in the face of human sin. Thank Him for His patience.

Her Name is Grace

Read Romans 3:21–26

For all have sinned and fall short of the glory of God, and are justified freely by his grace through the redemption that came by Christ Jesus. ROMANS 3:23–24

Grace, she takes the blame, she covers the shame
Removes the stain — it could be her name
Grace… it's a name for a girl
It's also a thought that changed the world
She travels outside of karma, outside of karma
What once was hurt, what once was friction
What left a mark, no longer stings
Because Grace makes beauty out of ugly things
Grace makes beauty out of ugly things
— *U2, "Grace"*

I like the band U2, and so I was intrigued when the lead singer Bono gave a book-length interview to journalist Michka Assayas.

In the middle of the expected quotes about his rise to prominence and the rigors of road life there's an intriguing exchange about grace! Assayas, not a Christian, asks Bono about his reputation for spirituality, and Bono answers, "The thing that keeps me on my knees is the difference between grace and karma." He continues:

At the center of all religions is the idea of karma. You know, what you put out comes back to you: an eye for an eye, a tooth for a tooth; or in physics, every action is met by an equal or an opposite one. The whole universe operates on karma, on reaping what is sown. And yet, along comes this idea called Grace to upend all that… which in my case is very good news indeed, because I've done a lot of stupid stuff. I'd be in big trouble if karma was going to finally be my judge. It doesn't excuse my mistakes, but I'm holding out for grace. I'm holding out that Jesus took my sins onto the Cross, because I know who I am, and I hope I don't have to depend on my own religiosity.

At this point his interviewer says, "The Son of God who takes away the sins of the world? I wish I could believe in that."

And Bono replies, "But I love the idea of the Sacrificial Lamb. The point of the death of Christ is that Christ took on the sins of the world, so that our sinful nature does not reap the obvious death. That's the point. It should keep us humbled… It's not our own good works that get us

What do you think the typical man-on-the-street understands better: Karma or grace? Why? How would you explain the difference between the two concepts?

How would you explain how God is able to be "both just, and the One who justifies"?

Express to God how thankful you are that He Himself balanced the scales by paying your debt!

through the gates of heaven." (*From Bono: In Conversation with Michka Assayas,* Riverhead Books*)*

That's precisely the theme of today's Scripture reading. It's literally a universal law that any action requires an equal and opposite reaction, and it applies spiritually in this way: Payment is required for our debt of sin.

You could call it "karmic" debt if you like, but the point is that there are echoes of our choices; in some way we can never fully understand, this sin-debt cannot simply be wished away. The scales must be balanced. As Bono says, it's a principle repeated in many world religions and etched on our very consciences.

And here's the really great news. The Bible says God Himself pays the debt: Jesus took the punishment for our sins. This is how God balances the scales, how He can be *"both just, and the One who justifies…"* (ROMANS 3:26) I love that beautiful phrase! *Only* God has both the power and authority to be simultaneously the One who is the source of all *justice*, and the One who *justifies* everyone who comes to Him. The sacrificial death of God Incarnate on the cross is the brilliant way He is able to be both merciful and holy at the same time.

Grace is free to us, but only because God is the One who paid the price. As you'll see tomorrow, Paul riffs on that concept for the rest of Romans, blown away by grace.

Hi, I'm René and I'm a Sinaholic

Read Romans 5:12–17

> *But there is a great difference between Adam's sin and God's gracious gift.*
> *For the sin of this one man, Adam, brought death to many. But even greater is*
> *God's wonderful grace and his gift of forgiveness to many through this other man,*
> *Jesus Christ.* ROMANS 5:15 [NLT]

Before I was a pastor, I was a disc jockey and also recorded voice-overs for commercials, promos, etc., for a variety of radio stations and other clients. Occasionally I'll still do some work in that area. I'll never forget one particular recording session: I'd been hired to record "liners," as they're called, for a talk radio station. Once the production director discovered I was also a pastor, he really let me have it! Every lame joke about pastors, every stereotype — the guy was relentless! I soon found out why.

"Look, I grew up in a church," he told me, "And every Sunday it was the same thing: 'Try harder to keep the Ten Commandments.' Well, it didn't work. I became an alcoholic. And I tried to stop. *But trying harder doesn't work.* The church message is a ridiculous lie. In my 12-Step group I finally realized that willpower is far from enough!"

Then he sat back and looked at me like, "I rest my case! I dare you to argue!"

I think he was pretty surprised when I agreed with him.

I told him that the moralistic message of many churches *is* totally misleading and very dangerous. The actual biblical teaching is not "try harder." It's that we are all sinners — *sinaholics*, if you like — self-destructive and deceitful.

Sin is not merely a bad habit to unlearn through willpower. We do sin willfully, but also, just like alcoholism, it's a disease. *It's not just that we're ignorant and need enlightenment. We are sick and we need a cure.* Today's verses mean no one's immune to the sin disease. We're all born with it. It's genetic:

> *For if, by the trespass of the one man, death reigned through that one man, how*
> *much more will those who receive God's abundant provision of grace and of the gift*
> *of righteousness reign in life through the one man, Jesus Christ.* ROMANS 5:17

That means that because of our disease, we were all destined for physical and spiritual death. The good news is, God gives us a cure! It's given to *"those who receive God's abundant provision of grace…"*

When did you think the message of the Bible or of your church was essentially "try harder"?

When and how did you begin to understand the message of grace?

Thank God for His "abundant provision of grace" through Jesus Christ!

Maybe you can relate to that production director. You heard things in church like:

"You have to try real hard."

"You need to give up this or that."

"Before God can bless you, you need to take this to the next level."

Mixed messages at best, emphasizing *what you do for God* instead of *what God does for you.*

Why don't such messages really work? We'll check that out tomorrow.

By the way, that production director was amazed at the biblical parallels to concepts he had learned in his recovery group and became a regular attender at our church, very enthused about *grace!*

Do Not Think of This!

Read Romans 7:7–25

OK, whatever you do right now DO NOT think of Sweet Tarts candy!

Absolutely *do not* imagine the feel of the round candies in your hand, the look of the pastel blues and pinks, the initial surprise of tartness when you put them in your mouth, the *snap* of the candy when you start to chew it, or that tangy taste in your mouth that makes those salivary glands under your tongue go into overdrive!

How're you doing on that? If you're like most people, your mouth is puckering up a little bit already!

All right, go ahead and think of Sweet Tarts but please, whatever you do, do not think of a nice roast beef dinner.

Do not imagine the creamy, buttery mashed potatoes on your plate, made just the way you like them, with rich gravy running over the mashed potatoes into that hot, perfectly cooked slice of marbled, rich, dark roast beef. Don't imagine how you smelled the aroma for hours as it cooked — and now you get to dig in! Of course this also means not thinking of that buttered bread roll melting in your mouth as you look down at the feast in front of you.

Some of you are just now picking this book back up again after disappearing for a snack following those first two paragraphs. It's almost impossible *not* to focus on something that you're reminding yourself not to focus on.

This is part of the problem with a legalistic system of righteousness. It's like telling someone not to think of a pink elephant.

As Paul points out in Colossians,

> *Since you died with Christ to the basic principles of this world, why, as though you still belonged to it, do you submit to its rules: "Do not handle! Do not taste! Do not touch!"? …Such regulations indeed have an appearance of wisdom, with their self-imposed worship, their false humility and their harsh treatment of the body, but they lack any value in restraining sensual indulgence.* COLOSSIANS 2:20–21,23

Note that Paul says such rules lack *any* value when it comes to really restraining impulses.

I watched an episode of Candid Camera where they put a sign that said "Wet Paint! Do Not Touch!" next to a park bench and then let the hidden cameras roll. And of course every single

Have you ever experienced the Wet Paint Effect: rules bringing out misbehavior? What happened?

What's wrong with the three unbiblical answers René mentions?

Ask God to help you focus on Him and His love instead of all the things you should not do! Start today by reviewing some of these devotions and the Scriptural truths in them, thanking God as you do your review for each blessing you have by grace!

person who saw the sign stared at the bench like they were overcome with bench-touch lust. They longed to touch it. They *had* to touch it! Touching that park bench became their controlling desire!! And how many people do you think wanted to touch the bench like that *before* someone put up that sign — or even thought about it at all? Exactly zero.

The Bible talks a lot about what you could call the Wet Paint Effect. It's not that the law is bad, but *focusing* on the rules of the spiritual life will often stimulate in you a desire for disobedience — not through any fault of the rules, but because of the way rules affect your sinful human nature. Paul talks about it in these verses:

> *But sin, seizing the opportunity afforded by the commandment, produced in me every kind of covetous desire… I found that the very commandment that was intended to bring life actually brought death.*
> ROMANS 7:8,10

So how can you get victory over sin in your life?

Three unbiblical but very popular answers:

1. *Moralism:* Just try harder to behave yourself according to certain standards.

2. *Legalism:* Put up extra "fence laws" to keep you from even getting close to breaking the law. For example, the command says "Do not commit adultery," so do not even *look* at a woman! In other words, even more *Wet Paint* to avoid.

3. *Anti-Nomianism:* Literally, "anti-law"; sort of like spiritual anarchy. The Law — and any other external rules — should be opposed by Christians in any form. This ignores the fact that the Law has its uses still.

If these are all bad ideas, then what's the biblical answer to changing your behavior? More on that starting tomorrow!

No Condemnation

Read Romans 8:1–4

> *Therefore, there is now no condemnation for those who are in Christ Jesus.*
> ROMANS 8:1

Back when I was really struggling with legalism my wife told me, "René, you are one of the most guilt-oriented people I know!"

It was true. I constantly felt guilty about not doing a better job as a pastor or a husband or a father or a friend, I felt guilty every time I messed up in any way, I felt guilty for past sins, and in those moments when I was happy, I quickly felt guilty that I *wasn't* feeling guilty! I can still slip into guilt-orientation to this day.

Maybe you can relate. Or maybe instead of that constant low hum of background guilt, there's one major sin in your past that keeps haunting you.

Well then, drink this in:

"Therefore..." Because of what Paul's been explaining in the Book of Romans.

"there is now..." Not there *will be*; not there *might be*; there is *now*.

"no..." Not there is *less*; there is *no*.

"condemnation..." In the original Greek language the word is *katakrimi*. The last part of that word, *krimi*, is where we get our English words "criminal" and "crime." It refers to a legal judgment about a crime in a court of law. Paul's saying there is no more sentencing, no verdict to wait for, no further penalty possible. The trial is over.

"...for those who are in Christ Jesus." Not for those who are perfectly well-behaved; not for those who fulfill certain religious requirements; for those in Christ.

What does it mean to be in Christ?

Experiment: Right now take a sticky note or 3×5 card, wrinkle it, write on it, bend it... and then place it in the middle of the pages of this book, without any of it sticking out. Then shut the book. Go ahead, try it. Notice what you see. Then come back and keep reading!

Done? So how much of the note's flaws did you see when it was in the book? None. Not because it did anything to clean itself — not because it tried hard — but because it was enclosed, encased, covered, by the book.

Do you really believe Romans 8:1? Why or why not? What would Paul say to you?

What does Paul mean in verse 3 when he says the law was "powerless"? What was it powerless to do? Why?

Thank God today for His total forgiveness! Offer to Him memories of past mistakes that may have been plaguing you. Ask Him to help you focus on His love instead of your sins.

That's what it means to be *in Christ*. It does not mean you have tried hard and earned credit for good behavior. It means you have received the free gift of His gracious covering of your sin.

I wish more Christians really believed this. There are so many emotional problems among Christians because they don't. They think God is angry with them continuously. They imagine that even when they try, God is saying, "You could have done better."

Bill Hybels said, "There are only two religions in the world: The religion of human achievement that asks, 'What must I *do?*' and the religion of divine achievement that says, 'Because of God it is *done.*'"

Do or *done*. Which religion are you?

For years, although I had been saying all the right words, in my heart I was really still in the first religion, trying hard to earn absolution. How did I finally get a sense of peace and security? That's tomorrow.

In the Grip of Grace

Read Romans 8:28–39

When I lived in San Diego my baseball hero was Tony Gywnn, so I could not believe it when he hit a foul ball directly into the stands exactly to the spot where my wife and I were sitting during a Padres game in the mid-1980s.

It was like the best gift ever, dropping out of the sky right into my hands. I didn't have to move, or even stretch — it came straight to me! I had literally dreamed of this moment, and now it was coming true!

I can remember every nanosecond of what happened next as if it is in slow-motion replay:

I see the bright blue Southern California sky. Here comes the white baseball, arcing right toward me in super-slo-mo. There's my hand, poised to catch it. Now into my field of vision enter… sixteen other hands, jostling mine as MY TONY GWYNN BALL comes soaring into the seats.

For one brief instant my fingertips graze the leather surface of my prize…

…then it bounces like a pinball off bumpers as everyone elbows for the elusive ball! It drops out of sight! I am dismayed as I imagine it skittering through the section! I scream in slow-mo, "NOOOOO!" Then… joy! I see it lodged firmly in the space between the hard plastic seat bottom and seat back of my wife's chair!!

I yell to her: "SIT DOOOOWN!!!!" And she does, plopping down on the ball, like a hen guarding her precious egg for her rooster-man. I begin to crow proudly in victory —

Until I freeze as I watch a foxy invader literally pluck the ball out from underneath my wife's… seat! Yes, unbelievably, a hand snakes down the seat back, reaches under her, and pops out that egg! She yells in outrage (OK, it honestly did sound a little like a chicken clucking in protest, just to complete the metaphor). The interloper has the ball and is high-fiving his seatmates.

For the rest of the game there was probably visible heat distortion above my head as I angrily contemplated how close I came to possessing a Tony Gwynn ball! Finally my wife (who had far more reason to be offended than I) said, "Cheer up, hon, you'll find a way to use this as an illustration!"

And I did! Here it comes:

How does it make you feel to know you are in the grip of grace?

When is it hardest to believe this is true?

What is your biggest question about what is taught in today's meditation?

Today pray through the Scripture reading and make it into a prayer of thanks to God! Imagine Him holding your hand firmly and lovingly.

Too often I think of myself hanging on to salvation like I tried to catch that slippery fly ball: I've got it one instant, but the next I could lose it! A variety of factors are always jostling me, robbing me, making it hard to be confident that I have what I seek.

But really, we are the ball, and the hand is *God's!* And we're firmly in God's grip, by His grace. He will never drop us. He will never let us go. He will never release his grasp.

I was thinking about this one day when I was walking along our local railroad tracks with my youngest son. The train tracks run right in front of a beachside amusement park and David was about three years old, an age when walking on the rails pretending to be a choo-choo is a better attraction than nearly anything inside the park.

Of course I knew he would stumble and fall (at that age they stumble and fall walking across a carpeted room), so I had his hand firmly in my grasp. Note: I did not just make sure *he* was holding my hand. *I* was holding *his*. There's a difference. His grip could slip; mine was firm. Because I love him.

Grace means more than your salvation. Grace means your Heavenly Father knows you will stumble, and knows your grip will slip… but *He* has you in *His grasp*. Because He *loves* you.

From predestination to calling to justification to glorification, we are in His grasp the whole way. So nothing *"will be able to separate us from the love of God that is in Christ Jesus our Lord."* (ROMANS 8:39). That's "the grip of grace." Still you may wonder, "If I am so secure, what motivates me to change and grow?" We'll look at that tomorrow.

Changed By Grace

Therefore, I urge you, brothers, in view of God's mercy, to offer your bodies as living sacrifices, holy and pleasing to God — this is your spiritual act of worship. Do not conform any longer to the pattern of this world, but be transformed by the renewing of your mind. ROMANS 12:1–2A

I took our youngest son, David, on a surprise trip to the Grand Canyon when he was 11 years old. Perfect day with blue skies, cool temperatures, and virtually unlimited visibility. It was so rewarding to watch his reaction when we drove right up to the rim and he stepped out to see this natural wonder for the first time in his life.

"Wow! Wow! Whoa!!!" he said over and over! Then we went on a hike into the canyon and made it to some amazing viewpoints.

Picture us negotiating narrow paths with sheer drops of several hundred feet; sunbathing on rocky promontories with world-class vistas in every direction; seeing the canyon colors change every few minutes from orange to red to purple to grey. It was stunning. David walked with me for a couple miles taking it all in, ooh-ing and aah-ing the whole way.

Now you have to understand that this is not the most outdoorsy, athletic child. This is someone who'd probably ask for a ride to his room if we could fit a car into the house. Yet he not only bounded along the trail with enthusiasm, he formulated a long-range plan. "Dad," he told me, "I have a new life goal. I want to go on a week-long Colorado River rafting trip and explore this place!" He's brought it up to me several times since then, too.

Know how many times I had to force him to hike a step further that day? Zip. He was propelled by awe. Did I ever have to tell him, "Think long-term and come up with a life goal that incorporates your experience today"? Nope. It was the wonder of the canyon that motivated him to exercise, to dream, to plan.

Sure, there was discipline involved; it was no picnic climbing back out of the canyon! But he truly did it with delight. His eyes were open to the spectacle he was experiencing. He couldn't believe it when I showed him on a map how far we'd gone. And when we called home he had such fun describing his day to the rest of the family.

Now compare that to running on a treadmill. How much hope do you think I have of getting David to hike on an exercise machine as far as he did that day at the canyon? It'll *never happen!*

How can the same exact things — Bible reading, prayer, evangelism — bring you joy or seem like drudgery? What makes the difference?

Well, the same effect applies to the disciplines of your spiritual life. If you live *"in view of God's mercy,"* if your eyes are open to grace, you'll want to give your life to exploring its depths with enthusiasm — and you'll feel enthused about inviting others to experience this supernatural wonder of the world.

But if you feel you're on a religious treadmill? Sheer numb boredom. Dry drudgery. Even resentment. It's in beholding Jesus and the wonder of His grace that we change, as Paul says:

> *And we, who with unveiled faces all reflect the Lord's glory, are being transformed into his likeness with ever-increasing glory…*
> 2 CORINTHIANS 3:8A

Are your eyes open to the wonder?

Have you been able to experience the spiritual disciplines, such as Bible reading, prayer, quiet time, etc., as times you actually look forward to? Why?

As Jerry Bridges says, "That is why we must preach the gospel to ourselves every day."

This is what it means in today's verses when Paul says to be transformed (the verb *be transformed* is in the passive voice — Paul is urging us not to *do* something, but to have something *done* to us) by the *renewing of your mind.*

It's sort of like positive brainwashing: Instead of the false messages from your culture ("You must be thin!" "You must become rich!" "You must prove your worth!"), you begin to hear and believe the messages from God's Word about the wonder of grace (*"You are blessed with every spiritual blessing" "You are a co-heir with Christ" "The same power that resurrected Christ is in you!"*).

The Grand Canyon's a wonder of the world, but spend time today thinking of the world's biggest wonder, God's grace toward you! Thank Him specifically for some aspect of His grace!

How are *you* trying to grow spiritually — by grace or by law?

An old poem attributed to John Bunyan puts it well:

> Run, John, run! the law commands
> But gives me neither feet nor hands
> Better news the gospel brings;
> It bids me fly and gives me wings.

THE TENSIONS OF GRACE

For sin shall not be your master,
because you are not under law, but under grace.

ROMANS 6:14

Can You Live With Grace?

Read Matthew 20:1–16

> *"Are you envious because I am generous?"* MATTHEW 20:15B

God's grace is so marvelous, so amazing, that you might wonder why anyone would ever reject it. It's a free gift, a grand prize better than the lottery! Why decline it?

Well… grace is messy, grace can seem unfair and illogical, and grace can be upsetting if I'm a prideful man (which I am). This week, let's look at some objections and tensions regarding grace.

I was reading blog comments the other day when I came across this insight by a woman named Marla Alupoaicei:

> Christians say that we want grace, but what we really want, deep down, is justice. We want the so-called "good people" of the world to be rewarded and the "bad people" to be punished. When we see the floodgates of heaven opened and God's grace poured out on the seemingly deserving as well as the undeserving, many of us act like the miffed older brother of the prodigal son or the laborer who worked the entire day for a denarius and grew disenchanted when he saw another worker receive the same pay for one hour's work.

You see this dynamic all through the ministry of Jesus: The good religious people are annoyed at the generosity of God. What about you?

Ever mentally *tsk–tsk* friends who spend way too much money on stuff you'd never buy? It's hard to remind yourself that it's not your money. The thing with grace is, *it's not your money*. And the One who has it is a big spender.

I guess you could say that's the hitch, if you've been looking for one, with grace: *You have to accept that others get it too.*

The very people you hate, the ones you loathe, the ones who drive too fast down your street, the ones whose loud parties annoy you at night, the ones who beg for money when you know it's a con, the ones who called you names in school, the ones who say they'll change but never do, the ones who hurt you so bad you still have scars, the ones whose politics you believe are leading the country to hell in a hand basket, the ones you disagree with on that litmus test issue, the ones who are ruining your city, the ones who let their dogs poop on your lawn, let their kids scream in church, let their impulses get out of control, cheated on you, lied to you, laughed at you, yelled at you, the ones who litter the beach, talk in movies, cut in line, the ones who flip

Do you agree or disagree with Marla Alupoaicei's statement? Why?

Is it hard for you to accept that a certain group or person can receive God's grace? Would it be tough to see someone in heaven? Who?

Thank God for being a big spender when it comes to grace! If there's someone you resent or have difficulty imagining "graced" by God, bring that person to God in prayer now. Ask God to soften your heart.

you off, cut you off, hack you off — well, if they simply receive it, they get grace too. Same as you. (And guess what? You might be on someone else's list!)

I think it was Groucho Marx who said, "I don't care to belong to a club that accepts people like me as members." That's something like the problem people can have with grace. If I get in, then anyone else can too. What if they don't deserve it?

As Philip Yancey writes, "In the realm of grace the word *deserve* does not even apply."

Can you live with that?

Drowning in Pride

Read 1 Peter 1:3–5

> *Those who cling to worthless idols forfeit the grace that could be theirs.* JONAH 2:8

I couldn't believe it. There I was, the youth pastor on one of my first trips to the beach with high school group since taking the job in San Diego… and I was drowning.

This was impossible. I knew how to swim. Growing up near the California coast, I'd been in the ocean more times than I could count. Yet I could no longer stay afloat.

I'd gone out on my own a half-hour before. Beautiful day. Just wanted to take a little dip. Then the rip current got me. Warning signs were posted on the beach, but I'd been out in conditions like that before and nothing had ever gone wrong. Well, it was going wrong now. I tried what I'd always been told: Swim parallel to the coastline; don't overdo it. Nothing worked: I was being swept further and further to sea, and I could feel my strength giving out.

Suddenly I saw my savior. He appeared right next to me — I didn't even hear him coming. He'd been keeping his eye on me, I guess, and saw that I'd been having trouble. The lifeguard put a flotation device around me and began swimming, first out of the rip current, and then straight to shore. And the only thing going through my mind? *"I hope no one in my youth group sees me!"* I was so embarrassed that I asked the lifeguard if he'd stop towing me in about 20 yards from the beach so I could swim the rest of the way myself, but he said no. I guess in a lifeguard's mind you're not saved until you're safe. Makes sense.

Once we got to dry land, I muttered "thanks," tried to stand up on weak legs, and just toppled over. Then I saw some kids from my group running toward me. And I turned away from my rescuer. I was too embarrassed to admit anything had been wrong or even to say thanks. Never went back to find him either.

I really don't like to tell that story because it reveals so much of my pride. I neglected to thank the lifeguard because of my pride. I almost short-circuited the rescue because of it. I ignored an important lesson I could have taught the kids because of it. That's a lot of pride. Reminds me of today's verse, written by a guy who knew something about rescue at sea.

Why would someone *"forfeit the grace that could be theirs"*? What would keep someone from receiving a free offer of rescue? It happens when you're too proud to take the help.

"What will my friends think?" has gone through many minds when considering Christ the Rescuer's offer.

Have you ever refused help because of pride? What happened?

Were you once too proud to receive the grace of God? How did things change?

Ask God to show you where you are proudly clinging to idols — of pleasure, of security, of any kind — and refusing His grace.

Or maybe they still think, "I can make it on my own," like a toddler who insists, "I do it myself!" or a teen whose favorite phrase is "I know!"

The problem is, this kind of thinking is drilled into us. In *Healing Grace*, David Seamands lists several barriers to grace related to pride:

1. Cultural barriers

Self-reliance may be the most dominant cultural value in modern society, expressed in clichés like: "I did it my way." "To thine own self be true." "Do your own thing." Just today at the checkout stand I saw these headlines on the cover of the (appropriately named) *Self* magazine: "Live the Life YOU Want to Live!" "Feel More in Control of EVERYTHING!"

2. Theological barriers

Many Christian churches believe in the doctrine of salvation by grace through faith, yet in the sermons and very atmosphere of the church there's not always a consistent message of grace. Instead, church attenders perceive an emphasis that goes something like, "Rise above; try harder; be better; improve!"

3. Family barriers

Your concept of God is largely formed by your relationship with your parents. You may feel your parents over-emphasized performance, forcing you to *earn* their affirmation, or on the other hand were so lax they seemed unloving.

The good news is that many of the Bible's authors had the exact same barriers! But God's grace still changed them as they stopped clinging to their pride.

Oh, and I learned something else the day I almost drowned: *In a Savior's mind, you're not saved until you're safe.*

When Jesus saves, He doesn't just save you part way. That's not salvation. He saves you all the way to shore — all the way to heaven. Like Peter says in the reading today, our salvation has both begun — and is yet to come. Once He's begun, your Savior won't stop until you're all the way home.

Vertical First

Read Matthew 22:34–40

Mark Galli recently wrote a great article for the magazine *Christianity Today* titled, "In the Beginning, Grace." His main idea is that churches — and individual Christians — desperate for growth are trying all sorts of things from programming techniques to "spiritual disciplines" to an emphasis on "social justice" causes, but they tend to forget one thing: *grace.*

He quotes Christian Smith and Melinda Lundquist Denton's book *Soul Searching: the Religious and Spiritual Lives of American Teenagers.* They conclude, "We have come with some confidence to believe that a significant part of Christianity in the United States is actually only tenuously Christian in any sense that is seriously connected to the actual historical Christian tradition, but has rather substantially morphed into Christianity's misbegotten step-cousin, Christian Moralistic Therapeutic Deism." It's moralistic, meaning it's all about improving your life through the application of principles; it's therapeutic, meaning it's all about helping you feel better; and it's deism, meaning it only vaguely believes in a higher power.

A lot of people have noticed this, but here's the trap: Galli observes that the many attempts to "deepen" the theology and practice of such Christians are still rooted in self-effort. He notes that even the "spiritual discipline" movement can be characterized by a focus on the self. And the social justice movement also can emphasize the horizontal dimension of life (how we care for those around us) at the expense of the vertical dimension (how we relate to God). I love the way he puts it, so I'll quote him here extensively:

> In short, we frame the problem horizontally. We focus on what we fail to do, and then talk about what we should do differently. To be fair, such solutions often start with a strong vertical dimension… But our practical and activist sensibility — one of our movement's stellar attributes — tends to undermine the vertical. This is the problem as I see it at the moment. The more mature leaders …know this spiritual reality all too well. They've watched too many activists burn out because they knew not the vertical dimension… But the language we use to describe our goals and to persuade others can so easily degenerate. A website that crystallizes the theology and goal of what I call the "following Jesus movement" says, "Following Jesus is … about a *lifestyle* of peace and justice *that sets one apart from others*" [emphases added].

In our righteous frustration lies a temptation that entices us when we start anxiously comparing ourselves with "others." This is the temptation of the devout that Jesus

Why do you think it is so easy — even natural — to slip from a vertical focus to a horizontal focus?

Why would a true vertical focus on God naturally demonstrate itself in a genuine horizontal love for others?

Today simply allow yourself to luxuriate in that vertical relationship: God loves you and lavishes grace upon you!

described, of the evangelical Pharisee who thanked God that he was no longer like sinners! …How easily the conversation slides into what *we* are doing.

…The place to begin is not more feverish doing…. The Word of God says the way to start working on the horizontal is to look up, in particular, at the one hanging on the Cross. The place to begin is not more doing but a type of non-doing….

At this point, the careful evangelical reader wants to know exactly what that looks like — "What should I *do* next?" …But the righteous desire to do something immediately to fix the problem of the horizontal is itself another symptom of the problem…

When we meet God in his paradoxical presence, we will once again know that great paradox of the Christian faith: with our focus on the vertical, when the weightlessness of belief becomes for us the weight of glory, that's when we are born again, born in the Word and *for the world*. This is something that happens once, yes, at one's conversion. But it also happens daily, at one's reconversion each morning and each Sunday. Then we become new creations, blessed with vertical life and energy and grace to do the horizontal thing we are called and gifted to do.

Even this Grace Immersion can turn into a horizontal rather than vertical focus: "Have I done my reading today? If I do all the readings and go to all the groups, will I then be magically set free from my bondage to performance-oriented religion?" The last thing I want is for you to feel any pressure to measure up to any of your friends or small group members when it comes to your appreciation of grace! To get back to a previously developed metaphor, all of these readings and verses are meant to be sails put up for you to catch the breeze of grace!

To really grow in an authentic, joyful way, just relax and enjoy the vertical dimension of grace first, and then allow that grace to overflow in the horizontal direction. As Jesus said, the greatest command is to love God. The second is to love your neighbor as you love yourself. That order is no accident.

Grace is Risky!

Read Romans 6:1–4

> *What shall we say, then? Shall we go on sinning so that grace may increase? By no means!* ROMANS 6:1–2A

Some Christians are afraid to really embrace grace. They object that people will just go ahead and sin like crazy. And maybe some will. That's a risk of grace even Paul had to address.

But if my message doesn't lead to the possibility of grace being misunderstood like this, then I'm probably not preaching grace.

D. Martyn Lloyd-Jones was a very rigorous, super-conservative scholar/pastor who taught at the legendary Westminster Chapel in London for many years. His sermon series on the Book of Romans is profound. Check out what he said about today's verses:

> The true preaching of the gospel of grace always leads to the possibility of this charge being brought against it. There is no better test as to whether a man is really preaching the New Testament gospel of salvation than this, that some people misunderstand it and misinterpret it to mean that it really amounts to this, that because you are saved by grace alone it does not matter at all what you do; you can go on sinning as much as you like… If my preaching and presentation of the gospel of salvation does not expose it to that misunderstanding, then it is not the gospel.
>
> I would say to all preachers: If your preaching of salvation has not been misunderstood in that way, then you had better examine your sermons again, and you had better make sure that you are really preaching the salvation that is offered in the New Testament… there is this kind of dangerous element about the true presentation of the gospel of salvation. (Quoted in Swindoll, *The Grace Awakening*, pp. 39, 40)

Ever since I enthusiastically rediscovered *grace* and started preaching it, I've heard some say I'm "soft on sin." I've heard that I don't care about spiritual disciplines. I've heard others say the opposite, that when I do an intervention and confront someone in our church about destructive behavior, I'm being inconsistent because I'm *not* showing grace. I had a man tell me that he could cheat on his wife because he was "covered by grace."

Not only am I willing to take the risk of being misunderstood like this; I know that when I am, I'm probably on the right track, because the Apostle Paul had to deal with these exact same

Do you agree or disagree with the Martyn Lloyd–Jones quote? Why?

Are any of the three symptoms of "grace abuse" above true of you?

Ask the Lord to show you if you've been using grace as an excuse for a lack of discipline, or blatant sin. Ask Him to remind you that though grace is free to you, it cost Jesus so much!

misunderstandings! Certainly legalistic teaching would *never* be subject to such misinterpretation.

On the other hand, here are some ways to detect if you're excusing sin with "cheap grace":

1. There's a lack of love and care about how your behavior affects others

2. There's a rationalization of blatant sin

3. There's an unwillingness to be accountable

There are warnings against this kind of "grace abuse" throughout Scripture:

> *Shall we sin because we are not under the law but under grace? By no means!* ROMANS 6:15

> *…godless men… change the grace of our God into a license for immorality…* JUDE 1:4

> *You are free… but don't use your freedom as an excuse to do evil.* 1 PETER 2:16 [NLT]

Why not? Well, Peter says, because *"you are a slave of whatever controls you."* (2 PETER 2:20B)

The point is, God loves you and wants to free you.

And just as legalism makes you a slave in one sense, sin makes you a slave in another. Whether it's sexual sin, substance abuse, laziness, gossip, anger, or anything else, you become a *servant* to it, following your master around as he leads you on a leash. You slowly lose control over your own desires and behaviors. Then your master begins to rob you of your health, your reputation, your relationships, your time, your motivation and more.

Now that you are free spiritually from the slavery of performance-oriented religion, why rush right back into another kind of captivity? Stay free!

No Brownie Points

God… has saved us and called us to a holy life — not because of anything we have done but because of his own purpose and grace. 2 TIMOTHY 1:8B

In his excellent book *Holiness By Grace*, Bryan Chapell observes how the idea that our good works will not earn salvation runs counter to our natural way of thinking.

He tells a joke about a guy who dies and faces Peter at the gates of heaven. Peter says, "Here's how this works. You need a hundred points to make it into heaven. You tell me all the good things you've done, and I'll tell you how many points they're worth."

The guy says, "OK, I was married to the same woman for fifty years and never strayed, not even in my heart."

"Great!" says Peter. "That's worth three points."

"Three points? Well," the man continues, "I attended church my whole life and tithed and volunteered!"

"Awesome!" says Peter. "One point."

The guy's starting to panic now as he blurts out, "Hey, I helped open a shelter for the homeless and I fed hundreds of needy people every Thanksgiving!"

"Right, that's two more points," says Peter.

"TWO POINTS!?!" cries the man, "At this rate the only way I'll ever make it to heaven is by the grace of God!"

"Congratulations," Peter says with a twinkle in his eye, "Come right on in."

The Bible says that God is no one's debtor (ROMANS 11:35). He is *God*; He doesn't owe anybody anything. Therefore, it's illogical to think that God owes me salvation because of my good works. It can *only* be by grace.

But this can be hard to take! Even the famous reformer Martin Luther wrote:

> The heart is always ready to boast of itself before God and say, "After all, I have preached so long and lived so well and done so much, surely He will take this into account." …But it cannot be done. With men you may boast, but when you come to God, leave all that boasting at home and appeal from justice to grace. …But let anybody try this and he will see… how exceedingly hard it is.… I myself have been

Why do our good works not make God love us more?

preaching… [the message of grace] for almost twenty years and I still feel the old clinging dirt of wanting to deal so with God that… He will have to give me His grace in exchange for my holiness. And I still cannot get it into my head that I should surrender myself completely to sheer grace; yet this is what I should and must do.

As Bryan Chapell points out, the hymn writer of the old song *Rock of Ages* got it right:

If that's true, then why do good works?

> Nothing in my hand I bring,
> simply to Thy cross I cling;
> naked, come to Thee for dress;
> helpless, look to Thee for grace;
> foul, I to the Fountain fly;
> wash me, Savior, or I die.

Make the lyrics of Rock of Ages quoted above into your prayer today.

Grace and Rewards

Set your hope fully on the grace to be given you when Jesus Christ is revealed.
1 PETER 1:13B

In the very last chapter of the very last book of the Bible, Jesus talks about heavenly rewards: *"I will give to everyone according to what he has done"* (REVELATION 22:12).

In the Gospel of Matthew, He promises that He *"will reward each person according to what he has done"* (MATTHEW 16:27).

The apostle Paul said the Lord *"will reward everyone for whatever good he does"* (EPHESIANS 6:8).

But doesn't the idea of rewards in heaven — for *"what we have done"* — contradict the idea of *grace*? You might be thinking, "Here I thought I was escaping performance-oriented religion with all this talk about grace — it's supposedly not about what I *deserve* — and now, in heaven, God brings performance right back into the picture!"

Someone emailed me this exact question:

> I've heard there are degrees of reward in heaven based on one's works on earth. I find this troubling. I could probably make an argument against it — it could lead to jealousy, greed, and prejudice in heaven! Plus I believe this could rob us of proper motivation for our works on earth, driven less by love and more by the *cha-ching* of the eternal scorecard.

But as Randy Alcorn explains in his extensive volume *Heaven*, rewards after death are simply *another expression of God's gracious nature*. In heaven God can no longer *save* you from sin by His grace or *sanctify* you by His grace, since you will then be perfect. So how will He express His *grace*, the *giving* that is such an essential part of His character? By continuing to lavish His riches on you in the form of *rewards!* See, God didn't have to *save* you. But He did. And He doesn't have to *reward* you. But He does. Why? Because you're so great? No. Because *He's so gracious!*

Let me make this clear: Your good deeds won't make God love you more. His love for you is *already at full strength*. But because He is *generous*, He loves to celebrate the smallest good deeds, like a father celebrates the smallest step his toddler takes.

And I mean the *smallest* steps. I used to think heavenly rewards would go only to the real ultra-saints. But look at what the Bible actually says about what God rewards: giving a cup of water to someone (MARK 9:41); giving to the needy, in any amount (MATTHEW 6:3–4); being mocked for your

Have you ever given a cup of water to someone, or visited someone sick? Imagine Jesus joyfully rewarding you in heaven for that deed, as He said He would. What is your response to Jesus?

faith (LUKE 6:22–23); inviting disabled people over (LUKE 14:13–14); and Paul even says you'll be rewarded for stuff you do at work — if you do it as if you're working for the Lord (COLOSSIANS 3:22–24). That's just a sample list, but I think the point is, just about *everything you do* can count for eternity. It's like God is looking for excuses to hand out rewards! *He just loves to be gracious.*

Another way to look at it: God is a gentleman. He says thank you. Maybe you do something for which you never get thanked. You visit someone in a nursing home who may not be capable of fully expressing gratitude. Or you're a faithful single parent, and you feel like no one has any idea how non-stop it all is. Well, God knows. And God can't wait to tell you, "I really appreciated that!"

Explain in your own words how the idea of eternal reward does not contradict the idea of grace.

So don't be discouraged. Set your hope fully on the *grace* to be given you when Jesus Christ is revealed (1 PETER 1:13B)!

Express to God your thanks that His grace will extend even to rewarding you for the smallest good deed. Praise Him for His grace! Ask Him to help you see needs for you to meet in a gracious way.

Does Grace Protect You?

The Lord has promised good to me.
His word my hope secures.
He will my shield and portion be,
As long as life endures.

Recently I met one of my writing heroes, sports journalist Rick Reilly. He was autographing books at a local store and by the time I reached him I was the last in line. So when I mentioned that I sometimes quote his columns in my sermons he had the time to seem intrigued (or at least polite!) and said he had a few questions for me about Christianity.

He told me how he had interviewed football superstar Isaac Bruce shortly after Bruce had survived a horrific car crash. Police at the scene said they'd never seen a sports car crushed like his, yet Bruce walked away without a scratch. But here's what upset Reilly: According to him, the athlete had attributed his survival to "calling on the name of the Lord" during the accident and went on to state unilaterally that if anyone claimed the name of Christ they would also be protected from harm.

Reilly looked at me and asked, "So do you think that if people pray to Jesus they're protected?" How would you answer that question? What does the Bible teach?

The first part of my answer: No.

God's saving grace does *not* mean nothing bad will ever happen to you. I've seen so many Christians believe this lie, and have their faith dashed. God's grace means He will *redeem* every hurt. Like the song says, He leads *through* the dangers, toils and snares, not *around* them.

After all, you follow a Savior who Himself was not protected from all injury. The very symbol of your faith, the cross, reminds you that Jesus — and many of His followers for the past twenty centuries — experienced painful death. But it also reminds you that God transformed the cross into a symbol of hope and triumph.

We are *sometimes* granted *healing* grace that takes away our pain; but we are *always* granted *sustaining* grace that strengthens us in our pain.

So, no, faith is not a guarantee you won't be harmed. As you'll read tomorrow, Paul said he begged God to take away his suffering, but God's answer was, *"My grace is sufficient for you, for my power is made perfect in weakness."* (2 CORINTHIANS 12:9) Grace guarantees God will *work for good* in every one of your sorrows. It doesn't guarantee there will *be* no sorrow.

In what area of your life do you sense that, for right now anyway, God is saying "My grace is sufficient for you, for my strength is made perfect in weakness"?

How in the world would it bring God more glory to work through some of your pain instead of simply eliminating all your pain?

How has God worked through weakness and pain in your life, both for your good and for others?

Thank God that He redeems the pain to bring good out of it. Thank Him for at least one specific way He has done that in your life. Then bring to Him any situation causing you pain now, and ask Him to either remove it or work through it to bring Him glory. Then rest in His grace, knowing He will answer in the best way.

However the second part of my answer is: Yes.

Ultimately, yes, God's grace does protect from *lasting* harm. Grace *guarantees* that He will work all things out to His glory, and *"there will be no more death or mourning or crying or pain."* (REVELATION 21:4) The pain now is a burst of static compared to the infinite celebration-song that awaits you. And God's grace is a *promise* you'll be there for the celebration!

Grace, in other words, *will lead you home.* As Peter promises:

> *And the God of all grace, who called you to his eternal glory in Christ, after you have suffered a little while, will himself restore you and make you strong, firm and steadfast.* 1 PETER 5:10

GRACE-INSPIRED CHANGE
Grace in Ephesians

Be kind and compassionate to one another,
forgiving each other, just as in Christ God forgave you.

EPHESIANS 4:32

Identity Change

Long, long ago he decided to adopt us into his family through Jesus Christ.
EPHESIANS 1:5 [THE MESSAGE]

I was so burned out by my obsession with performance and my drift into legalism that I knew *that* wasn't the secret to living a changed, Christian life.

But when I started getting into the concept of grace, my old performance mentality sounded some major alarm bells: If I really owned the idea that I was forgiven and accepted totally by grace, wouldn't I just sin like crazy? The fear of punishment had been my major motivator, so was there a better alternative?

One author has a great way to illustrate this. Imagine a kingdom where the king decreed that all prostitutes and thieves in the land would receive a royal pardon. Great news if you're a prostitute or a thief. No more worries about your criminal record. No more anxiety every time you see a police officer. But you wouldn't necessarily be motivated to change your lifestyle. In fact, maybe you'd even use the pardon as an excuse to continue your reckless behavior.

But now imagine that in addition to the pardon, the monarch came to a prostitute personally and asked her to be his wife. She'd be the queen, the royal representative of the kingdom. Would she be motivated to change? How could she not be?

Or imagine the king picking a thief off the streets and adopting him as a prince, the heir to all the riches of the kingdom. Why would that guy ever go back to thievery when he's now a zillionaire?

Well, the Bible describes you as part of *"The Bride of Christ,"* the church. It also says you've been adopted into the family as an heir. Both descriptions mean that your identity has been altered.

When you became a Christian, you probably believed that because of the sacrifice of Christ your sins were forgiven. But do you understand that you are now also an heir, a bride, with all of the love and all of the riches of the Great King lavished on you? How could I have missed this? It's a teaching throughout the Bible:

> *How great is the love the Father has lavished on us, that we should be called children of God! And that is what we are!* 1 JOHN 3:1A

> *Now if we are children, then we are heirs — heirs of God and co-heirs with Christ…*
> ROMANS 8:17

Would you say most Christians are focused on sin (even trying hard not to sin), or are focused on their newness of life in Christ? Or something else? Why? What about you?

How can the concept of my new identity — given to me as a gift by God, not earned — help me change my behavior?

Thank God today for bringing you into His family. Pray for Christians who do not see themselves this way yet — that their eyes would be opened to the truth! (See Paul's prayer in Ephesians 1:15–19) Read Romans 6:13 and make it into a personal prayer as you offer each part of yourself to God as an instrument of righteousness.

You are not a slave, but a child… And if you are a child, you're also an heir, with complete access to the inheritance. GALATIANS 4:7 [THE MESSAGE]

So this week we'll focus on erasing and replacing the old tapes playing in your head ("I am a loser!" "I am destined to disappoint and fail!" "I am a reject!") with new tapes ("I am a child of the King!" "I am the royal representative of the new kingdom!" "I have a God-given role and destiny!").

For true internal (and not just external) change it is *vital* to keep reminding yourself of the vast riches lavished on you by God's grace. This is why the Apostle Paul starts most of his epistles with a wonder-filled meditation on the generosity of God. He is putting the horse before the cart when it comes to change — first you need to really have your eyes open to your blessed status; only then do you find motivation and inspiration to live a changed life!

I heard someone say it's like taking away a toddler's favorite stuffed animal. That kid is going to scream because he's focused on what he's losing. Now imagine replacing that stuffed animal with a puppy: The toddler's got a new focus now!

That's what you could call *the grace method* to overcoming sin. We are focused on what we've gained; our previous lives we count as loss. In other words, instead of saying *"Do not sin,"* Paul's message is *"Live freely!"*

I'm not saying you'll be a sinless, perfect person. But I guarantee you'll spend less fruitless time wallowing in guilt and delayed by perfectionism, and more time being an ambassador for the kingdom and relaxing in the serenity and peace that come from living a new, righteous life!

The Treasure You Already Have

Read Ephesians 1:3–23

> *In him we have redemption through his blood, the forgiveness of sins, in accordance with the riches of God's grace that he lavished on us with all wisdom and understanding.* EPHESIANS 1:7–8

William Randolph Hearst invested a fortune in collecting works of art for his fabled home, Hearst Castle. The story goes that one day he read about some valuable pieces of art he just *had* to have. So he sent his art agent to Europe to find them. The agent looks high and low. Months go by. Finally he returns to California and reports to Hearst that the items have at last been found – but that Hearst absolutely cannot purchase them. Hearst is furious. "Name the price!" he says, "I must buy them!" "I am sorry sir," the agent answers, "but that is impossible!"

Hearst is confused until the agent explains why: *They're already stored in his own warehouse.* Hearst had purchased them years before! He'd owned them all along but was still seeking them, because they were hidden away, out of sight.

What a parallel to the way many Christians live! We have the riches of every blessing from God already "lavished on us" as Paul says in today's reading, but many of us are still out looking for them! That's because our riches, like Hearst's art, are often hidden away, out of sight. It's not that we don't have God's blessings — it's just that we have forgotten! We need to frame them and display them — remind ourselves daily of our spiritual wealth!

Some of the riches you already own…

- *You have every spiritual blessing already* (EPHESIANS 1:3) Will you believe this or keep trying to earn what is already yours?

- *You're holy and forgiven in God's sight* (EPHESIANS 1:4) I can't count the times I prayed "Please forgive me!" forgetting that I had this treasure already!

- *You've been chosen by God* (EPHESIANS 1:4,11) Forget the debate over the words "chosen" and "predestined" for a minute and realize Paul's pastoral point: You are part of a people with a destiny. Will you believe this?

- *You're God's masterpiece* (EPHESIANS 2:10) You're a work of art! You have a purpose: to do great things God has already lined up for you to do! Will you believe this or keep looking for approval and validation elsewhere?

Why do we Christians forget about the treasure we already have?

Which of the bullet points is most difficult for you to believe? Easiest? Why?

Go through Ephesians 1 and thank God specifically for the many things that are true of you — by His grace!

This is just the tip of the iceberg! And don't forget it's all *"to the praise of His glorious grace, which He has freely given us in the One he loves"* (EPHESIANS 1:6).

That's why Paul says, *"I pray also that the eyes of your heart may be enlightened in order that you may know …the riches of his glorious inheritance in the saints"* (EPHESIANS 1:18).

Here's an action step: This week, read the bullet points on the previous page of this devotion every day!

See, it's when you understand the lavish grace you *already have* that you stop vainly trying to justify yourself, and begin to *really change* from the inside-out, as we'll see tomorrow!

The Gospel According to LOST

Read Ephesians 2:1–10

> *For it is by grace you have been saved, through faith — and this not from yourselves,*
> *it is the gift of God — not by works, so that no one can boast.* EPHESIANS 2:8–9

For six years the TV show *Lost* spun the yarn of several plane crash survivors on a mysterious island somewhere in the South Pacific. This masterfully made series captivated the imaginations of millions, including me.

The last show was an excellent parable for what passes for Christianity — or at least spirituality — in America today. In the afterlife the show's characters all gather for passage into some sort of heaven. They meet in a place dominated by Christian symbolism: there are several shots of a statue of Christ; a character leading them is named "Christian Shepherd"; they sit in church-like pews… and there are also many symbols of other religions. But the real point of the episode is revealed in several comments about how characters had *redeemed themselves*.

As Maureen Ryan, the TV columnist for the *Chicago Tribune*, wrote, the last episode was "a testament to what the show was about: creating your own world. Creating your own fate." She went on:

> Sorry to get all religious on you, but… these lyrics came to mind:
>
> > Amazing Grace, how sweet the sound,
> > That saved a wretch like me.
> > I once was lost but now am found,
> > Was blind, but now I see.
>
> They once were lost, but now they're found. They got to leave on their own terms. It just felt true to the show and [its] themes: It's never too late. You can always remake your fate. No one is eternally good or bad. You can… redeem your character through your actions.

She's right about the themes of the show, and I found it interesting they reminded her of 'Amazing Grace." But the song doesn't say "*I* saved a wretch like me." It says "*Amazing grace* saved a wretch like me." The *Lost* finale was an emotionally moving demonstration of what you could call America's pop culture religion: You may be "lost" but you can save yourself and go to heaven if you're good enough.

It's all so close to what the Bible teaches that a Christian friend asked me the day after the *Lost* finale, "That's not what we believe… is it?"

How would you describe the way our popular culture believes we get to heaven?

How would you describe the Bible's teaching?

Thank God that you did not have to depend on your own works to get you to heaven, but were saved by the grace of God through faith in Jesus Christ! Ask God to help you spread that good news!

Well, I do think that's *exactly* what a lot of us believe, but that's not what the *Bible teaches*. Biblically, the lost are more like drowning people who *can't* save themselves. In fact, the Bible puts it in even starker terms: Before God's grace rescued you, you were *dead*. How much can a dead man do to save himself? Absolutely zero.

So why do we seem to want to believe we can redeem ourselves? In today's passage from Ephesians — which reads like a summary of the whole book of Romans — the Apostle Paul implies this way of thinking gives me reason to "boast": It makes me feel good about myself!

At first it's soothing and hopeful when I believe I can turn my life around. It's inspiring, in a self-help, Horatio Alger "Go west, young man!" kind of way, except the cry is, "Go to Heaven, young man!"

Three problems:

1. In real life, willpower doesn't work for long, not even with my fate in the balance.

2. Self-effort can lead to discouragement. I'm *never sure if I'm doing enough* to merit redemption.

3. Self-effort leads to subtle pride. I begin to measure myself against what others are doing.

This last effect is the most dangerous of all. Pride has poisoned everything we humans have done here on earth, especially religion. *The only way for human pride not to taint heaven is for salvation to come as a gift of love from a gracious God.*

I still loved the *Lost* finale, but I know this: I once was lost, and when I go to heaven it will be because the true Christian Shepherd found me and will lead me home!

Transforming Grace

For you were once darkness, but now you are light in the Lord. Live as children of
light (for the fruit of the light consists in all goodness, righteousness and truth)…
EPHESIANS 5:8–9

"This church is so different!" the woman rushed up after the worship service to tell me. Whenever I hear that I think, "Oh, no. This person just doesn't know us that well yet! We're full of the same kinds of knuckleheads — including me — as every other church!"[1]

But as I listened further she went on: "As a kid I was dragged to a church that preached 'hellfire and brimstone' sermons. I left every service feeling guilty and condemned. But I've been here for the last two months, and I love how the preaching's positive and upbeat!"

Again I was cautious and asked, "So how do you see God changing your life here?" I guess I was worried she saw us as a generic positive-thinking church that endorsed anything and everything.

"Well, *everything* about my life has changed," she said. "If I can just be real candid, I have stopped sleeping around. I start and end every day with Bible reading and prayer and I *love* it. I'm in the women's Bible study here. And I even stopped smoking pot!" Honestly I was stunned and stammered out something like, "Uh — I don't remember preaching about pot lately!"

She laughed, "I know! But my first week here I prayed to receive Jesus into my heart, and that day I went home and just *knew* what I had to do!"

Now I don't want to give you the impression it *always* happens this way, but you need to know that I see this sort of thing more often than not. I also do not want to give you the impression that this woman is now sinless and will have no further struggles. But when you *get* grace, you begin to change *internally*. Once you feel *free*, you don't want to be a *prisoner* again, neither to legalism nor to sin.

I was seeing in that woman's life exactly what Paul talks about here:

> *"Therefore, as God's children, holy and dearly loved, clothe yourselves with*
> *compassion, kindness, humility, gentleness, and patience."* COLOSSIANS 3:12

I used to see this as meaning, basically, "So since you're Christians, act like Christians!" But that's not exactly what Paul's saying here, is it?

[1] Sorry if you attend our church and don't think you're a knucklehead, but, hey: I call it like I see it.

How does an understanding of grace help give you a lasting motivation for changing the way you live?

What is one positive way your understanding of grace has changed your behavior?

Today pray, "Thank you Heavenly Father, that I am Your child, holy and dearly loved! Let me be as gracious to others as You have been to me."

Zoom in on the phrase "dearly loved." You are loved. *Dearly* loved. By God Himself! He has made you His child! *Everything Paul says next is grounded in this act of grace.*

Now you are compassionate… because you understand how infinitely compassionate God is to you. Now you are kind… because God's kindness to you has led you to repentance. Now you can be humble… because you know you have not done anything to earn God's love. Now you can be gentle… because God was gentle with you. Now you are patient… because you are aware of how amazingly patient God has been and continues to be with you.

And this is extremely, world-changing-level important: notice how Paul doesn't really give out various religious rules in these verses when he describes the life of a Christian — he is describing *character traits* that develop in a heart that has been "graced."

Funny thing is, that woman's "hellfire and brimstone" childhood church probably preached the exact same biblical morality our church preaches. But they apparently used *guilt* as a motivator, not *grace*. One problem with guilt motivation: It only lasts as long as the guilt. So to keep people motivated, pastors in churches like that one have to keep preaching guilt.

Grace, though, never ends! It is infinitely fascinating and rewarding, as long as you stay focused on Jesus and not your own efforts.

If I Get Grace, I'll Get Gracious

Read Ephesians 4:17–24

One under-taught aspect of the doctrine of grace: If you've received grace, it should be making you *gracious*. In fact, Christians, if they are really immersed in their doctrine of grace, will be the most gracious people on the planet!

Our world needs this!

Columnist Martin Smith asks, "What social pathology explains the reluctance of so many people to pull over for passing funeral processions, to make small talk with fellow passengers, to exchange the pleasantries that for generations helped lubricate social discourse?"

Ours is a combative, aggressive, vulgar culture. But the kingdom of God's culture is a gracious, forgiving, beautiful one. And we, as its ambassadors, should reflect that culture to everyone we meet.

John Vawter wrote a great book about this called *Uncommon Graces*. He talks about listening well, treating people with gentleness, showing mercy, and being kind. This kind of graciousness opens people's hearts to hear the story of a gracious God.

In his book he talks about how Andy Rooney, the commentator from *60 Minutes*, got into a New York taxi one day. He expected the typical New York abrasiveness from the cab driver, but instead he got a cheerful "Hello!" and a warm smile. And that was just the start! The driver was gracious and talkative during the whole trip.

It was such an unusual experience that before he got out of the cab, Rooney asked the guy why he was so polite and courteous.

"I'm out to change New York!" the driver said.

"But… you're just one guy," said Rooney.

"I know, but I figure if I show kindness to you, you'll show it to the next person you meet, and they'll pass it on to someone else. It'll be like a big, expanding ripple, spreading out through the whole city!"

That's a guy with vision about the power of graciousness!

There *is* a ripple effect and that's one reason 1 Peter 3:16 says to share your hope *"with gentleness and respect, keeping a clear conscience."*

How are you at being gracious? To whom is it most difficult to be gracious?

How does your graciousness level reflect an awareness of God's grace?

Thank God today that He is compassionate and gracious, slow to anger, and abounding in love. Ask Him to help you be like that too — starting with your next interaction today!

Gracious behavior helps pave the way for the doctrine of grace.

Psalm 103:8 says that God is *"compassionate and gracious, slow to anger, abounding in love."* These characteristics of a gracious God can be reflected in you!

But does being grace-filled toward others mean I'm a mealy-mouthed weak-willed pushover? Does it mean I'm always mumbling apologies? More tomorrow!

Grace-Flavored Speech

Read Ephesians 4:25–31

Today let's investigate the impact of grace on your speech. By the way, one handy guide to understanding Paul's epistles: Paul's epistles! He often summarizes what he means about any given topic in his own, shorter epistles. Thus much of what he says in Romans is summarized in the shorter Ephesians, and much of what he says in Ephesians is summarized in the even shorter Colossians. One example: You could say Paul has a pithy summary of what he says in Ephesians about the use of words in Colossians 4:6:

> *Let your conversation be always full of grace, seasoned with salt, so that you may*
> *know how to answer everyone.* COLOSSIANS 4:6

I love that phrase: *"Let your conversation be always full of grace."* It reminds me of a slogan I saw in Hawaii: "Spread the aloha spirit." Spread the *grace* spirit! How? As always, Jesus is your guide.

Think of Jesus and the Samaritan woman (JOHN 4). When she says, *"I have no husband,"* Jesus could have attacked her for her immorality (turns out she has had several husbands and is not married to the guy she is living with) but instead He compliments her for her candor!

Think of Jesus and the woman caught in adultery (JOHN 8). By all rights, He could have condemned her. Instead He reminds everyone in the crowd that they too have sinned — and then says to her, *"Neither do I condemn you."*

Think of Jesus and Peter after the resurrection (JOHN 21). He gently restores him with the question, *"Do you love me?"* and then the simple phrase, *"Feed my sheep."*

"Full of grace" means "gracious" and "graceful" speech, but it means more than that. As James Montgomery Boice points out, the way Paul uses the words in this verse could also mean "let your conversation be full of the doctrines of grace." In other words, "Let a lot of what you talk about be God's grace." What an encouraging subject!

Now think of conversations you hear in our society, on radio talk shows, or at work or school. Too often they're full of insults, seasoned with sarcasm; or full of judgment, seasoned with self-righteousness; or full of anger, seasoned with crudity.

As poet Maya Angelou said on the *Today* show:

> There is a blight in American society which has taken root in our souls and in our
> mouths: Vulgarity. Whether it comes from white shock-jocks or black hip-hop artists,
> vulgarity demeans people, robs them of dignity. How have we come to this place?

Rudyard Kipling said, "Words are, of course, the most powerful drug used by mankind." What kind of "word-drugs" are we using in our culture today: Words that heal, or words that addict and destroy? How so?

Do you agree with Maya Angelou's comments? Why?

How would you complete this sentence: "My words tend to be full of _____, seasoned with _____?"

Again, ask God to help you show grace specifically through your words for the next 15 days!

What about you? Let's start a movement to change vulgar language and *harsh* language to *grace-filled* language. As part of this Grace Immersion, try this: For at least the next fifteen days, until the end of this study, *only* speak grace-filled words. After all, Paul says to let your conversation be *always* full of grace. That means more than just good manners (although that's included!).

Seven ways to fill your conversation with grace:

1. Stay away from vulgar or harsh words (like cursing).

2. Be encouraging. Praise others regularly. Be specific with your encouragement.

3. Tell people you love them.

4. Smile and look into the eyes of anyone you talk to.

5. Offer mercy at every chance. Be quick to forgive.

6. Remind people of God's love for them.

7. If you need to correct or offer suggestions, do so with a gentle, grace-filled spirit. Speak the truth in love, but never gripe or complain.

Do this not as a duty; do this as a response to God's grace to you! In simple terms: You *give* the grace you *got* from God!

The Grace Immersion means more than just learning about grace. It's about really *immersing* yourself in a grace-filled lifestyle, and your words are part of that immersion!

As Justin Taylor puts it, "We think words, hear words, speak words, sing words, write words, and read words — all the time. Every day." So the words you choose to use will shape your life and the lives of others more than almost any other single factor.

Free to Forgive

Read Ephesians 4:32–5:9

> *Be kind and compassionate to one another, forgiving each other, just as in Christ God forgave you.* EPHESIANS 4:32

Our family travelled to Uganda this year to visit relatives who live there. One night in Entebbe we went to a fantastic wood-fired pizza restaurant right on the beach owned by a Rwandan woman, Goretti, married to a Dutch diplomat (Classic! An Italian restaurant run by a Rwandan married to a Dutchman living in Uganda!). She has an amazing story. Living in Europe when the genocide began in Rwanda, she returned to find 63 family members had been killed. How could she go on after that tragedy? She says, "You must forgive, or your life is over."

These sorts of stories about radical forgiveness intrigue me. What motivates some to seek revenge while others spread mercy?

Perhaps the most haunting snapshot of the Vietnam War was a widely publicized photograph of a little girl running naked down the street, screaming in pain. She was burning from the effects of a napalm bomb. The girl was Kim Phuc. Years later, as a grown woman she was a guest of honor at the Vietnam Memorial on Veteran's Day. She laid a wreath at the monument and then gave a short speech: "As you know, I am the little girl who was running in the famous picture… I have suffered a lot from both physical and emotional pain… but God saved my life and gave me faith and hope."

She told how, in the moments after the attack, the photographer who took her picture brought her to a hospital. Years of painful burn therapy followed. Later the Vietnamese government sent Kim to Cuba to study. There she met and married Bui Huy Toan, a Christian, and became a believer herself. On their way home from their honeymoon in Moscow the couple defected to Canada, where they now live with their son. Their goal is to go back to Vietnam to share the gospel of grace with their people.

At the Veteran's Day ceremony, Kim publicly forgave the unknown pilot whose load of napalm seared her skin and killed her grandmother and two younger brothers: "Even if I could talk face to face… I would tell him we cannot change history, but we should try to do good things for the present and for the future to promote peace."

At that point, according to newspaper accounts, many of the veterans present began to openly weep.

Have you found it easy or difficult to forgive others?

Is there someone you need to forgive?

Bring to God any grievances you hold. Ask Him to help you show grace as you have received grace. Ask God to help you not receive His grace in vain. Ask Him to help you know how to show radical grace to others in a way that is wise and godly.

The more amazed you are at God's grace to you, the more you'll find yourself inspired to give grace to others. This is such an important result of grace that Paul says in 2 Corinthians:

> *As God's fellow workers we urge you not to receive God's grace in vain.*
> 2 CORINTHIANS 6:1

What a haunting sentence! What does he mean, *"receive God's grace in vain"*? In the previous verses we see the specific context: This is about forgiving a brother who sinned.

Earlier in the epistle Paul talks about how the Corinthian congregation had put out of its fellowship a person who had done something terrible — it may be the same man Paul discussed in First Corinthians who was openly living in sin with his own step-mother. In any case, a man had committed some kind of sin, had been put out of the fellowship, and had now repented.

Paul wants the church to receive this guy back, but the church leadership is apparently unwilling. They're suspicious of his motives and mindful of his past. But then Paul says in Christ we're all new creations; *"the old is gone, the new is come."*

Then in 2 Corinthians 6:1 Paul says he fears that the Corinthians have essentially received God's grace *"in vain"*; that is, they *believe* in God's grace for *themselves* but apparently it is not *changing their hearts* to the point they are willing to extend grace to *another*.

What about you? Are you still stingy with forgiveness even after it's been richly lavished on you? Are you secretly annoyed that God will probably forgive someone more easily than you might? Anyone who hasn't done quite enough to receive your mercy?

I have had to wrestle with this myself. For years I felt white-hot anger whenever I thought of the man who molested me when I was his 9-year-old piano student. His identity was lost to our family after all those years, but I still fantasized vengeance periodically. I had to learn to give my hurts to God and release anger that was only poisoning me. This decision began a process of healing in my life that truly set me free.

RIPPLE EFFECTS OF GRACE

So then, just as you received Christ Jesus as Lord,
continue to live in him.

COLOSSIANS 2:6

Grace Fuel

Read Colossians 2:6–12

> *So then, just as you received Christ Jesus as Lord, continue to live in him.*
> COLOSSIANS 2:6

This is a great time in our Grace Immersion for a reminder: You don't learn about grace and then move on to other, deeper doctrines in order to really mature as a believer. You mature only by remaining focused on the infinite riches of God's grace to you, even as you study other facets of the faith.

This was brought home to me the other day when I proved once again that I am not exactly an automotive expert. In the latest of several car-related fiascos, I successfully (but unintentionally) disabled yet another vehicle.

Our executive pastor Mark Spurlock was headed out for the day when he realized his car's gas tank was on absolute empty. He'd coasted into the church parking lot that morning and had of course forgotten all about it until it was time to go. Being the ever-helpful senior pastor and friend, I said, "Hey, I remember seeing a gas container down in the bus garage!"

We found the container and poured its contents into Mark's tank. Brilliant! We had shown ourselves to be resourceful problem-solvers. I waved good-bye from the parking lot as he drove out to the street in his car. Which then sputtered. And backfired. And coughed. And died.

"Hmmm. Maybe there's a fuel pump problem," I growled, trying to sound like a real car guy. We just couldn't figure it out though and ended up calling the man who drives and maintains our church bus. He came over, took one look at the container from which we'd poured gas into Mark's car, and doubled over with laughter. Turned out the two genius pastors had poured *diesel* gas into a *normal* engine. Apparently you're supposed to continue running your car on the same kind of fuel you started with. Who knew?

Paul says in today's verse "*…just as you received Christ Jesus as Lord, continue to live in him.*" This one verse could save so many running-on-empty Christians a lot of grief. You *start* your Christian life on *grace* fuel. But if you're like most, you often try to *continue* on *works* fuel. And then you get perplexed: How come I'm running out of gas when I've been pouring so much into the tank?

The problem isn't that you're not showing initiative or not trying hard. In fact you're pressing on the pedal as hard as you can. The problem is that it just doesn't work. *You're using the wrong fuel.*

What distractions or substitutes are there for simple faith today?

What do you think it means to continue in Christ just as you received Christ?

Ask God to help you begin today to live in Jesus just as you received Jesus.

We start our faith life singing "Amazing Grace," but then we often *continue* by singing "Working on a Chain Gang," which could have been the soundtrack for the Colossian church.

It was under siege by false teachers who taught that Jesus had a role to play, but there were also many extras to add to the spiritual to-do list. It's "Christ Plus" thinking: Jesus is okay, but I need some extra spiritual secrets and practices. Paul says, no, just stick with a simple focus on Christ and His grace.

Sadly, most Christians think the doctrine of grace applies only to salvation. It's for spiritual newbies to get *started.* The reality is, grace is for *every moment* of your Christian life. You need *grace* to face trials, *grace* to know how to treat others, an appreciation of the *riches of grace* to deal with discouragement, a *grace focus* to change your sinful behavior…. So *start* on grace, and *keep living* that way!

As you'll see this week, the ripple effects of this kind of life will touch everything and everyone around you.

Giving Grace

Read 2 Corinthians 8:1–13 *(Notice how many times the word grace is used!)*

> *But just as you excel in everything — in faith, in speech, in knowledge, in complete*
> *earnestness and in your love for us — see that you also excel in this grace of giving.*
> 2 CORINTHIANS 8:7

Famine has come to Jerusalem. Christians are starving.

Meanwhile, Paul is traveling and decides to encourage the churches he's visiting (in what is now Turkey and Greece) to take up an offering for the suffering people back in Jerusalem, partly because he sees this as a great chance to show that they are all one in Christ! Remember, the Greek and Roman Christians had been viewed with suspicion by many of the Jewish Christians, so he's thinking this act of charity could go a long way toward mending bridges. The Christians in the wealthy city of Corinth get excited and pledge their support!

Problem: They then sort of… forget. So in today's verses Paul has the awkward duty of reminding them that they need to give that money since he already told the Jerusalem Christians that it was on its way!

It's fascinating to see: How does Paul motivate them to do this?

He doesn't nag, or beg, or scold, or guilt-trip them into anything. He motivates them to give through *grace*.

He talks about how much grace God lavished upon them. He talks about the gracious giving and the resulting joy that he has seen in others. And then he makes very clear that they are to give because it is an *act* of grace, in *response* to grace.

It's intriguing to me that Paul says the *Macedonian* churches had followed through on their pledges already, *although they were in extreme poverty themselves,* while the rich Corinthians had lagged behind in their giving even though they were wealthy.

I read some statistics showing that, in the United States, those below the poverty line give about 5% of their income, those in the middle class give about 7% of their income, while those who are in the highest income brackets give less than 2% away. Of course there are extremely generous wealthy people (I am privileged to know many who are a great example to me), but if these stats are to be believed, generally the very poor apparently give a higher percentage than the very rich.

How could you "excel" in the grace of giving?

Ask God to help you overcome any latent stinginess and excel on the grace of giving, just as He has been gracious to you!

Maybe that's because the very poor have a more immediate personal understanding of the need for grace — and the blessing of grace — while the wealthier are often better able to maintain an air of self-sufficiency.

That's why Paul encourages these wealthy Corinthians to *excel* in the grace of giving, just as the poor Macedonians had been doing.

In other words, the *grace of giving* is something we're to practice, something we're to grow in, to expand on. It's one habit we are told to indulge!

How can you do this? I think it's a good idea to have regular "grace projects" through which you stretch your own generosity muscles. Check out our list of ideas on page 155.

This way you *"grow in grace"* practically, not just theologically!

Sometimes the grace of giving means working to set the oppressed free from a giant evil in society, as we'll see tomorrow.

Freedom Fighter

Read Luke 4:14–21

One fascinating part of the "Amazing Grace" story is how the song's writer, John Newton, ended up campaigning against the very slave trade he'd once helped lead.

Newton's chance to fight slavery came in 1788 when, after years of debate, British Prime Minister William Pitt finally formed a committee to investigate the slave trade. The star witness — and the only man in England who was willing to paint the harrowing details of that practice as an "insider" — was Newton.

In his pamphlet *Thoughts upon the African Slave Trade* Newton summarized his testimony:

> Silence would, in me, be criminal. I hope it will always be a subject of humiliating reflection to me that I was once an active instrument in a business at which my heart now shudders…

> I should think it rather unsuitable to my present character as a minister of the Gospel to consider the African slave trade merely in a political light… The righteous Lord loveth righteousness, and he has engaged to plead the cause of the oppressed. I ought not to be afraid of offending many, by declaring the truth, if indeed there can be many who plead for a commerce so iniquitous, so cruel, so oppressive, so destructive, as the African Slave Trade!

Newton did not just revel in his own position as a man forgiven by God's grace. He also did something about the "ungrace" toward others he saw in his society. He celebrated his spiritual freedom and also worked for both spiritual and physical freedom for the oppressed, seeing this as part of his calling.

It's intriguing to me that the primary social causes Newton encouraged in his young followers were: making the slave trade illegal; passing laws against cruelty to animals; and reforming manners, including vulgar language. You could say that each of these causes was about bringing *grace* to situations where "ungrace" prevailed.

Jesus announced the start of His earthly ministry by reading a prophecy about Himself from the book of Isaiah:

> *The Spirit of the Lord is on me, because he has anointed me to preach good news*
> *to the poor. He has sent me to proclaim freedom for the prisoners and recovery of*
> *sight for the blind, to release the oppressed, to proclaim the year of the Lord's favor.*
> LUKE 4:18–19

How can you help bring grace to part of your world or neighborhood that is "ungraced"?

Why is this often hard?

Ask God to help you live as a child of light! This means both seeking personal holiness and freeing oppressed and poor people around you.

Notice that the message of grace — the good news of God's favor — is intertwined with helping the poor. In its original context in Isaiah this verse is part of a section that clearly teaches that we're to help the poor, the oppressed, the hungry. It's part of bringing God's grace to a world that needs it!

When you're set free by grace, you're not given this gift just so you'll feel better. You're called to *"live as children of light"* (EPHESIANS 5:8) in a world of darkness.

But remember, you don't do this to prove anything to God. He already loves you unconditionally.

As I heard someone say, "I do this not from mere *motivation*; I do it from *inspiration!*" The more you understand the grace of God, the more you'll long to extend that grace in every way. As you saw earlier in this Grace Immersion, the horizontal result of grace follows the vertical reception of grace.

Group Grace

Read Galatians 6:1–5

Carry each other's burdens, and in this way you will fulfill the law of Christ.
GALATIANS 6:2

It's almost 10:00 p.m. as I write this. I've just returned from a meeting of the 12 Step group that meets at our church. I was inspired to visit in part by Philip Yancey's visit to the recovery group at his church described in *What's So Amazing About Grace?*

I love these groups. For one thing, they're such a great example of carrying each other's burdens. No one's judged for being an alcoholic, addict, whatever — in fact the meetings start with introductions that go like this: "Hi, I'm (name), and I'm an alcoholic." And everyone responds in unison, "Hi, (name)!" It's the kind of transparency that should be born of grace.

When it was my turn to be introduced, I said, "Hi, I'm René, and I'm a churchaholic," and everyone laughed even though I wasn't really joking. I don't blame them, though, because it did sound kind of funny coming from a pastor. But as I already described, for years I was addicted to what I call "Churchianity."

Anyway, at every 12-step meeting a group member shares, and that night a woman about my age told her story. She said I could share it here. You might relate.

Sexually molested repeatedly as a child, she made pacts with God: "If I promise to behave, you will make this stop." Only it didn't stop.

"I thought I obviously wasn't perfect enough, because if you're good, then life gets good, right? So I tried harder," she told the group. "Then I gave up because it was too hard, and I went the other way, into sexual promiscuity. Since the pressure of perfection was too much, why bother even trying?"

She was a pregnant teen and "completely lost, when someone invited me to church and told me about Jesus. I said I could never come to Christ because of how bad I was. But this man said I could just come as I was — and I did, and found unconditional love for the first time in my life." She discovered amazing grace.

I wish I could tell you that her story after that was a long ride into the beautiful sunset, enjoying God's love every step of the way. But that's not how it was. A few years later at that same church she found her life's purpose through being a foster mother. Starting in her twenties, she helped

Can you relate to the woman's story? In what way?

raise nineteen kids that way — tough kids the system had almost given up on. Most turned out okay but, when a few remained troubled, she blamed herself.

"Again I figured if I were a better Christian, I'd see better results. I had never worked that out, so I translated every message I heard at church and every verse I read in the Bible as 'Be Better!' I thought if I was only better, then everything would be blessed."

What was the flaw in her "religious" thinking — what did she believe about why good and bad things happen?

Over the next twenty years she slowly forgot God's grace and became performance-oriented again. Eventually this pressure contributed to a nervous breakdown, and a wise counselor suggested she try the 12 Step group. "I thought, 'What do I have in common with a bunch of drunks?!' I'm a good church person!" She came reluctantly, agreeing to a six-week commitment. That was over two years ago and she and her husband attend every week now. She says, "In the group I never feel I have to pretend to be someone else, someone better. I'm more at home with the alcoholics and addicts than the 'good' church people now!" Funny, that sounds a little like Jesus to me.

Why do you think 12 step groups have a level of honesty that "normal" church small groups can sometimes lack?

She not only rediscovered grace, she discovered how important it is to experience what you could call *group grace* — grace in *community*. I think it's possible for everyone in a church to express the same kind of honesty and care that the people in her group do. It is risky, though, and that's why people usually shy away from recovery group-style honesty. But some things are so awesome they're worth the risk!

At the conclusion of her story she shared with the group some truths from the book of Lamentations that have helped her daily bathe in God's grace:

Ask God to help you plug into a small group community — maybe a recovery group or a small group or a friendship circle — where you can find, and help build, an unconditionally loving "group grace" culture.

> *The LORD'S loving-kindnesses indeed never cease,*
> *For His compassions never fail.*
> *They are new every morning;*
> *Great is Your faithfulness.*
> LAMENTATIONS 3:22–23

Grace Frees Me To Be Honest

Read 1 Corinthians 15:9–11

> *Therefore, since through God's mercy we have this ministry, we do not lose heart.*
> 2 CORINTHIANS 4:1

How can grace help me become as candid and non-defensive about my character defects as the people in the support group we met yesterday?

In *Healing Grace*, David Seamands retells the fascinating story of a man named Stypulkowski, a fighter in the Polish underground resistance movement in World War II. As the war ended he was captured by Russians along with 15 other freedom fighters and made to stand trial for "war crimes," accused falsely of helping the Nazis. Prior to trial the men were tortured and interrogated in order to break them so that they would confess to anything.

The most effective interrogation technique was a form of blackmail. The torturers relentlessly accused the men of all sorts of behavior — in their work, their sex lives, their families — and when they found each man's weakness, they exploited it, threatening to tell the world of his sin if he did not confess to at least some war crimes and go to prison for a while. "Save yourself and your family a lot of shame," they would advise.

The men's wills, weakened by a starvation diet and sleep deprivation, all broke… except Stypulkowski. He was the only one to plead not guilty at the trial, and then, largely because of the foreign press covering the trial, was set free. He had been interrogated twice daily for 70 days, but he kept his Christian faith alive through daily prayer. And it was his understanding of God's grace that seemed to make him immune to the threats. As David Seamands writes:

> Oh, it was evident that he was not free from weaknesses — his accusers pointed them out to him time after time — but he was never shattered by them.

> He daily presented himself to God and to his accusers in absolute honesty…
> So whenever they accused him of some personal wrong, he freely admitted it,
> even welcomed it.

> He said, "I never felt it necessary to justify myself with excuses. When they showed me I was a coward, I already knew it. When they shook their fingers at me with accusations of filthy, lewd feelings, I already knew that. I said to them, 'But gentleman, I am much worse than that.' For you see, I learned it was unnecessary for me to justify myself. One had already done that for me — Jesus Christ!"

Do you tend to be self-defensive or secretive about your shortcomings? Why or why not?

In today's verses Paul shows this same confidence: *"Since through God's mercy we have this ministry, we do not lose heart."* He knows he doesn't have his ministry because of his performance. He has no illusions about his "goodness." He knows it's all by grace. *"By the grace of God I am what I am..."* That's why he doesn't lose heart.

And so it is with you.

Why is it important for your personal character growth for you to understand that all you have, you have by the grace of God?

When you truly realize that everything you have is by God's grace, you'll find the courage for total honesty about your shortcomings and needs, and experience healing grace.

But how does grace help me navigate the often prickly personalities and hot controversies I encounter everyday? That's a great, often-forgotten ripple effect of grace that we'll look at tomorrow.

Thank God today for all you have by the grace of God — take a few minutes to specifically list in prayer some of the blessings for which you are grateful.

Grace To Disagree

Read Romans 14:1–10

> *Who are you to judge someone else's servant? To his own master he stands or falls.*
> *And he will stand, for the Lord is able to make him stand.* ROMANS 14:4

Someone called our church office last week wanting to know our "official position" on a non-essential issue. You'd be surprised how often I'm asked for our "position." I'm asked by people in the church, people visiting the church (who presumably want to be reassured that they are among fellow enlightened beings), members of the media… in fact I'd say I'm asked about our stand on *non-essential* issues more than I'm ever asked about our stand on the *essentials* of the faith!

Well-known pastor and author Chuck Swindoll says he's deluged with these requests. Why? As one woman wrote him, "How are we to know what to decide on this issue if Chuck doesn't tell us!?"

I'm glad it's his policy not to make official pronouncements on such things. Of course many other pastors are only too delighted to oblige! But you will never mature as long as you have to get your opinions on everything from some leader.

In Romans 14, Paul explains how to get along by grace without all the uniformity enforced by legalism:

> *The man who eats everything must not look down on him who does not, and the*
> *man who does not eat everything must not condemn the man who does, for God has*
> *accepted him… One man considers one day more sacred than another; another man*
> *considers every day alike. Each one should be fully convinced in his own mind…*
> *So whatever you believe about these things keep between yourself and God.* VS. 3, 5, 22

His big idea? "Let us therefore make every effort to do what leads to peace and to mutual edification." In other words, focus on the essentials, not the controversies. Why not be about the "one Lord, one faith, one baptism" instead of the latest litmus test issue?

As C. S. Lewis said, "When all is said (and truly said) about the divisions of Christendom, there remains, by God's mercy, an enormous common ground."

Read the gospels and the epistles carefully: What is the *one issue* that Jesus and Paul are willing to press? In a word, it's *grace*. They seem to raise their voices only when the legalists encroach

Why do you think it's sometimes hard for church people to agree to disagree on non-essential issues?

What surprises you about Romans 14?

Ask God to help you discern between essentials and non-essentials. Ask Him to help you extend grace to others, especially on the non-essentials.

on the gospel. They are silent on so many of the issues that were important to the religious people of the day.

Three keys to gracefully disagreeing:

1. *Don't demonize people who disagree with you.* Don't put a black hat on all your opponents. I bet many of them love Jesus just as much as you do — maybe more! It's horrifying to hear what can be said — in churches! — when people disagree. Instead, be gracious.

2. *Concentrate on things that cultivate peace and help others to grow.* Don't focus primarily on things that would be good controversial talk-show topics! Commit yourself to encouragement.

3. *As Swindoll says, "If you don't get your way, get over it and get on with life."* If you didn't get your way at a church vote or staff meeting, get over it. Don't keep replaying the scene in your mind.

I know it's not always easy, but make grace the message people see in your *actions* toward other people, as well as the cornerstone of your *doctrine*.

Saying Grace

Read Matthew 6:5–15

> *And when you pray, do not keep on babbling like pagans, for they think they will be heard because of their many words. Do not be like them, for your Father knows what you need before you ask him.* MATTHEW 6:7–8

When I was living with a performance-oriented mindset nothing was more contaminated than my prayer life. I figured if I prayed longer, earlier, more earnestly, with more spiritual words, then I'd please God more and get more positive answers! On my knees? Even better. Flat on my face? How spiritual of me!

Reminds me of the old joke: Two boys staying with their grandma kneel beside their beds one night to pray. First the older son prays briefly about how much he'd enjoyed the day. Then the younger son starts, but he prays much louder than his brother, practically screaming as he requests a long list of bikes and toys. When he's finally finished the older brother asks him, "Why were you praying so loud? God's not deaf!" and the younger one answers, "Yeah, but grandma is!"

Well, I was praying as if I had to break through God's deafness or inattention.

I honestly think I got this idea from the parable of the unjust judge in Luke 18:2–5. The Bible says Jesus told this story so His disciples would *"pray and not give up"* (v. 1). But I wrongly interpreted it to mean that God is like the judge: not really interested in my problems, but if I pester Him enough He'll hear me. So I spent hours on my knees. I thought I might, as Bill Hybels puts it, "wear Him down and wrench a blessing from His tightly closed fist."

But a parable is not an allegory, where every single element means something else. Instead it's more like a joke — a story with a punch line, only in the case of the parables it's a punchy truth. The truth here is that if even an unjust judge will respond to a politically unimportant person's repeated request, then *how much more* does your loving Heavenly Father hear you.

But you are not like the widow, and God is not like the judge. First of all, you are not poor and abandoned like the widow — *you are* the beloved child of God and a co-heir with Christ! Second, God is not like the judge at all — He's not crooked or uncaring or indisposed, but righteous and loving and always available.

This is the misconception behind legalistic prayer that Jesus corrects in Matthew 6. You are not heard *"because of your many words."*

How would you summarize what Jesus teaches about prayer in Matthew 6?

How can you avoid the trap of performance-oriented prayers?

Try the Lord's Prayer model today: First pray the very words of that prayer, with meaning. Then use it as a pattern for a prayer in your own words — express adoration, surrender, gratitude for grace, and request strength to be gracious to others.

So how should you pray? The Lord's Prayer that follows is a great model of prayer that really is saying grace.

First, it's short. About 50 words. That implies total confidence that God is listening. No babbling to impress God here.

Second, it starts with the words *Our Father*. Never forget you're a child praying to a Father who couldn't love you more than He does right now.

Third, it's a prayer of surrender. *Thy will be done*. It's not all about you.

Fourth, your needs are expressed simply: *Give us this day our daily bread*. No begging or bargaining. Why do that with a gracious God?

And fifth, it reminds you to give grace like you desire grace: *Forgive us our debts as we forgive our debtors*.

Nothing will revitalize and relax your prayer life more than really saying grace! And in prayer and meditation, instead of endless requests, you'll spend more time in contemplation of the really moving wonder of God's grace! That starts tomorrow!

THE WONDERS OF GRACE

From the fullness of his grace
we have all received one blessing after another.

JOHN 1:16

Approaching God with Confidence

For we do not have a high priest who is unable to sympathize with our weaknesses, but we have one who has been tempted in every way, just as we are — yet was without sin. Let us then approach the throne of grace with confidence, so that we may receive mercy and find grace to help us in our time of need. HEBREWS 4:15–16

Many mornings right around 5 AM, our cat Oreo meows loudly for her breakfast. She has decided that she does not like the stale cat food in her bowl; she wants new food, fresh from the box! For some unfathomable reason, I, the only person in the family who is regularly annoyed by our cat, am also the only one who ever hears our cat.

So around 5:01 I yank open our bedroom door, lurch out in an attempt at menace, catch Oreo's gaze with an angry bloodshot stare from underneath my alarming shock of morning Einstein hair, then make loud mewling noises that I sincerely hope sound to her like cat curses. I do all this with the kind of humorless intensity found only in someone awakened from a sound sleep. At 5:02 she sees me, arches her back, rockets up the stairs, and shoots through the cat door to safety in the garage. And then I go back to bed fuming. This happens *every day*.

When I next see Oreo I know what will happen: She will slink away from me, apparently embarrassed of her daily offense, or afraid of what I might do to her — or both (either way I'm sort of OK with it). It's incredible: She crawls around in something approximating guilt and fear *every morning*, yet with each new day she yields to the temptation again. Sound like someone you know?

Ever feel like God's going, "Not again!" after you fall? Ever feel like you don't dare come to Him in repentance because you fear what He'll do to you? Ever worry He'll be as crazily offended as I am when the cat awakens me from a sound sleep?

Bryan Chapell tells the story of a pastor's daughter who brought home a teddy bear made of chocolate from school. The next day the girl's mother caught her three-year-old son chomping down his sister's bear. The boy backed against the wall like a cornered criminal, sobbing his confession with telltale chocolate stains all over his mouth and hands. His Mom told him that, despite all his tears, he would still have to tell his sister what he had done when she got home from school that day.

That afternoon was torture for the little boy as with each passing minute he wondered how his sister would react. Finally she walked in. He ran to her as the dam of his guilt burst out in tears of confession. He cried, "Sally, I am SO SORRY I ate your teddy bear!!"

When you fall, do you slink around in fear and remorse, or do you approach the throne of grace with confidence?

I'm glad that his sister was always looking for a way to love her little brother. She took him in his arms, kissed him, and said, "It's okay, Johnny, I will love you forever and always." Though he was still crying, the little boy began to giggle. He was still crying from shame, yet at the same time he began laughing for joy.

What a great picture of grace. When I see how serious my sin is, I'm broken to the point that I cry tears of grief. But I don't need to be afraid of God! When I realize God says, "I will love you forever and always" and reaches down and in compassion embraces me, I cry tears of joy.

Why would God want us to know we can come to His throne with confidence, instead of slinking around in fear and guilt?

I love today's verse from Hebrews 4:16. It means that even when you fall, you can approach God's very throne — which the writer calls *"the throne of grace"* — with *confidence* because you *know* you will find *mercy* and *grace* to help you in your time of need!

As Dean Merrill puts it, "The good news to those who have made a major mistake in their lives is this: *It's okay to run to your Father."*

With confidence today, approach the throne of grace, knowing you will receive mercy and grace to help you, and tell God what you need.

The Panorama of God's Grace

Every good and perfect gift is from above, coming down from the Father of the heavenly lights. JAMES 1:17A

I've been talking mostly about saving grace and sanctifying grace, but as David Seamands says, that's like going to the Alps and only seeing the Matterhorn. There's so much more to inspire awe. I love his phrase "the panorama of God's grace." Let's look at some of the other wonders of grace.

General Grace

James says in today's verse, *"every good and perfect gift is from above...."* Everything true and beautiful and good in the world is a gift of God — it doesn't have to be explicitly religious or biblical for you to enjoy it.

The wisest man who ever lived, Solomon, said to enjoy your food and drink and family (ECCLE-SIASTES 9:7) because they are part of God's favor.

The Bible says *"whatever is true, whatever is noble, whatever is right, whatever is pure, whatever is lovely, whatever is admirable — if anything is excellent or praiseworthy — think about such things"* (PHILIPPIANS 4:8).

It doesn't say *religious* things that are lovely and admirable, etc. It says *whatever*. This means that there are landscapes, stories, music, knowledge, sports, and many other excellent and praiseworthy things you can experience with a joyful heart. Some examples for me: Reading *The Lord of the Rings*. Running on cliffs overlooking the ocean. Hiking in a redwood forest. Use wisdom and discernment and learn to enjoy God's general grace all around you all the time.

Christian musician Todd Agnew writes:

> The goodness of God is found in a ray of sunshine in the middle of a day of rain. His gift of joy even reaches through our darkest pain. In short, every little bit of goodness in my life originated in the heart of my God. Every thing that made me smile. Every ounce of beauty that caught my eye. Every color, every giggle, every cloud, every shower, every touch, every taste came from Him. He is the source of all good things, the fount of every blessing, the giver of ten thousand charms.

Like John says, *"from the fullness of his grace we have all received one blessing after another"* (JOHN 1:16).

What "admirable, noble, excellent, praiseworthy" examples of God's general grace do you love to enjoy?

Why is it important to remind yourself that God gives you good gifts to enjoy?

Today, spend some time drinking in the grace of God through His general gifts of beauty and truth. While you do, praise Him for His grace through this!

This is an idea taught by respected Christians throughout history. Even the very strict theologian John Calvin taught that God's general grace can be perceived through nature, as well as in "mechanical arts… liberal sciences… and even heathen philosophers and poets… all truth is from God, and if wicked men have said something true and just, we ought not to reject it, for it has come from God."

Let's look at some more peaks in the panorama:

Restraining Grace

If God allowed the consequences of human sin to run unchecked, we would probably have destroyed ourselves by now. Instead, because of His love and grace, He restrains some of the practice of sin (2 THESSALONIANS 2:7), withholds some of the consequences of sin (PSALM 103:10, ACTS 17:30), and gives us the idea of government and law enforcement to suppress the human tendency to self-destruction (ROMANS 13:1–7).

As I write this, our city is still cleaning up its downtown area after a Saturday night riot left scores of businesses vandalized. Ever wonder why this doesn't happen more often? I believe it's due to restraining grace.

Seeking Grace

The parables Jesus told in Luke 15 show God as a seeker of the lost. Not only do we love Him because He first loved us; we *seek* Him because He first *sought* us. My friend Rigo Dicochea shared his journey to faith one day in church and said, "I remember researching information about other religions and finding that *Christ found me rather than me finding Him.* I don't know if that makes sense, but… it just happened. He became my hope… my King."

When you decide to turn to Him, you find that what you thought would be a long trek back is really just one step — because He's been following you the whole time and is right there next to you! You turn around, and, whoa! there He is. As Paul tells the Athenians, *"He is not far from each one of us"* (ACTS 17:27).

Ultimate Grace

The amazing thing to me about heaven is that *even there, God's grace continues.* I mean, really, you're already in heaven; how much better can it get?! As I mentioned earlier, because *grace* is an essential part of God's character, even there, in the new heaven and new earth, in a perfect environment where we will want for nothing, He continues to *give.*

Sustaining Grace

Read 2 Corinthians 12:7–10

But he said to me, "My grace is sufficient for you, for my power is made perfect in weakness." Therefore I will boast all the more gladly about my weaknesses, so that Christ's power may rest on me. 2 CORINTHIANS 12:9

My father-in-law, Paul Ettinger, was shot.

He'd been chairing a meeting of the homeowner's association in his senior citizen neighborhood near Sun City, Arizona when a disgruntled former resident came in armed to the teeth and opened fire on the board members and everyone else in attendance.

Paul's first indication that anything was out of the ordinary was when he saw bits of paper floating through the air in front of him. He thought, "Why is someone throwing confetti at a time like this?" Then he looked down and saw the neat, round hole right between his first and last names on the nameplate on the table. And then he traced the path of the bullet through the stack of papers in front of him — the source of the "confetti" — right into his chest. Then he fell over.

As he lay on the ground bleeding, Paul heard more shots and then shouts. He discovered later that a small elderly man who had been standing in the back of the room had taken a chance and rushed the gunman, remembering his high school football training to "hit 'em hard and hit 'em low!" As soon as the surprised gunman toppled over one of the other retirees in the room yelled, "Get him, boys!" By the time police arrived the murderer was trussed up with rope from the supply closet and yelling for mercy.

After my father-in-law recovered fully from his wounds I asked him what he felt and thought during that time. He told me, "I was not afraid at all, and that surprised me. I felt the presence of God. I knew I was going to be OK, no matter what happened." My mother-in-law, June, echoed that statement. "I am normally such a worrier," she remembered, "But I just felt the presence of God like a comforting blanket. I just knew He was with us and things would be all right."

She said in all the chaos the only prayer she could think to pray was, "Jesus help us," over and over. "And I knew He was hearing that simple prayer," she told me. "It was almost a physical sense of His presence, as if He was right there next to me."

What my mother- and father-in-law experienced was God's sustaining grace. This is another peak in the panorama.

When and how have you experienced the sustaining grace of God in time of trouble?

Bring to God a tough time you are experiencing — and pray for someone you know going through a tough time too. Ask for God to richly bless with His sustaining grace!

God promises you His presence, not a trouble-free existence. In fact He warns there will be trouble. Jesus said, *"In this world you will have trouble"* (JOHN 16:33). That's a promise. You have His word on it.

Keep reading, though. Jesus then says, *"But take heart! I have overcome the world."*

That implies that just as Christ received grace to help Him in His time of need, so will you! And just as Christ ultimately overcame the world through His resurrection, you will too — by the promise and power of God's grace.

Super-Lavish Grace!

It's amazing to me now how I once thought of God as stingy.

I saw Him as a Zeus-like grandfather sitting on the clouds and only reluctantly releasing His blessings upon those He deemed worthy.

But when grace revolutionized my life, my perspective changed. I hope you see now that the Bible describes God as having limitless generosity, and that generosity is summed up in the word *grace*. It's used 150 times in the New Testament to describe God's favor bestowed on undeserving people — people like you and me!

The Bible says we're saved by grace (EPHESIANS 2:8), and by grace we stand through life's difficulties (ROMANS 5:2). Jesus is described as *"full of grace"* (JOHN 1:14) and the one who gave us *"grace upon grace"* (JOHN 1:16). Paul talked about God's *"abundant grace"* (ROMANS 5:17), and *"surpassing grace"* (2 CORINTHIANS 9:14). Peter called it *"multifaceted"* grace (1 PETER 4:10), the literal meaning of the Greek word *poikilos*.

The super-lavish nature of grace really comes home in Second Corinthians:

> *And God is able to make all grace abound to you, so that in all things at all times, having all that you need, you may abound in every good work.* 2 CORINTHIANS 9:8

That one verse summarizes everything you need to know about the whole arc of grace: God provides it to begin with; and God continues to give all the grace you need at all times, so that you overflow with grace to others through your good works! You truly are immersed in grace!

Realizing the extravagant riches of God's grace can motivate and uplift you every day!

The famous London preacher Charles Spurgeon rode home one night after a hard day's work feeling exhausted and discouraged. Then he thought of the verse, *"My grace is sufficient for you"* (2 CORINTHIANS 12:9).

He said that immediately into his mind came the picture of a tiny fish in the mighty Thames River, afraid of drinking too many pints of water lest the river be drained. Then Father Thames says to him, "Drink away, little fish. My stream is sufficient for you."

Then he thought of himself as a tiny mouse in a massive grain silo in Joseph's Egypt. And Joseph says to him, "Cheer up, little mouse. My granaries are sufficient for you."

Finally he thought of a man exercising, dreading that his breathing will exhaust the oxygen in the atmosphere. But the Creator's voice booms out of heaven, "Breathe away, oh man, and fill

What difference will it make in your life if you believe God is lavish with His grace?

Thank God for His lavish grace. Think of some specific ways He shows grace to you each day!

your lungs. My atmosphere is sufficient for you!" (Spurgeon story adapted from John MacArthur, *Our Sufficiency in Christ*)

I hope you let yourself breathe in, feast on, bathe in, the lavish riches of God's grace that are poured out on you every minute! Grace is something in which you are meant to *luxuriate!*

Grace in 3-D

Read Romans 5:17–20

Ever stare at one of those computerized 3-D posters that were all the rage a few years ago? They look like randomly colored pixels without any discernible pattern until you relax your eyes. Then a three-dimensional image snaps into focus! The one I stared at in the mall had a cool picture of a flying eagle, but it took a while for me to get the hang of seeing it — and I'm sure I looked completely goofy as I swayed back and forth in front of the store window, cross-eyed, trying hard to make some sense of what was right in front of me (very much like I appear every morning before my first cup of coffee). But I discovered that what seems disorganized and random eventually becomes amazing and majestic (I mean the poster, not me).

That's what happens to the Bible when you relax and focus on grace. You start to see the whole book as one giant 3-D picture.

First God lavished His grace on us with a perfect world in Genesis 1. It's all good. Then we humans spoiled it when we sinned. But God was gracious and promised a future redeemer, setting the plot into motion! Then we humans kept messing up — even though we were given God's perfect law, thereby proving we can't save ourselves, even with an owner's manual.

Yet God was merciful and forgave the repentant, even coming to earth as the incarnate Son of God. Jesus could have spoken out against many evils in society, but His primary target was religious legalism, which clouds and perverts the message of God's grace.

Then humans killed the Son of God. But God is stunningly gracious and in an amazing plot twist, turns even that tragedy into triumph: The death of Christ turns out to be the very way God had planned to pay the debt for all of our sins Himself. And the cross switches from a symbol of punishment and death to a symbol of grace and life. In fact the crucifixion and resurrection are a microcosm of the whole story: There is no tragedy, no sin, beyond redemption by God. Sin is trumped by grace again and again, in every life!

Then at the very end of the story, there's a vision of the new heaven and new earth. Once again, God lavishes His grace on us with new life in a perfect sinless world. The circle is complete. And there's one final invitation to receive grace:

> *The Spirit and the bride say, "Come!" … Whoever is thirsty, let him come; and whoever wishes, let him take the free gift of the water of life.* REVELATION 22:17

Have you taken the free gift of the water of life by receiving Christ?

How does it make you feel to see the story of grace traced throughout the Bible?

Thank God for His story of grace — one that He began writing thousands of years ago, and continues writing on your heart and life today! Pray about how you can play your part and keep telling the story to others!

See the 3-D picture yet? Maybe this will help your focus: I love *The Message*'s paraphrase of Romans 5:18, 20:

> *Here it is in a nutshell: Just as one person did it wrong and got us in all this trouble with sin and death, another person did it right and got us out of it… Grace, because God is putting everything together again through the Messiah, invites us into life — a life that goes on and on and on, world without end.*

The Bible, in other words, paints a cohesive picture with each small story — and as your eyes see it coming into focus you'll see God turning to *you* even as you stand looking at the picture, and inviting you to be part of His masterpiece, the picture He is painting for the whole universe to see, the portrait of His grace!

Calming Grace

Read Psalm 103:1–12

Bryan Chapell tells about his son Jordan in his book, *In The Grip of Grace*. Jordan is apparently one of those high-energy toddlers who is destined to be something like a stunt man in Hollywood. He is a risk-taking daredevil.

Yet Brian says one of his favorite snapshots of Jordan was taken inside a hotel room after a day of amusement park fun and sightseeing on a family vacation. In the picture, Jordan is sleeping in his mother's arms.

> To understand the significance of this picture, you have to understand… the kind of day we had before the picture was made. When the time finally arrives for him to rest after such a day, it is no easy task to settle Jordan down. But my son has a wonderful mother, and she has discovered the secret of calming him when things seem on the verge of pandemonium.

> Kathy takes Jordan into her arms and tells him about his birth.

> She says, "Oh, Jordan, when you were born we were so happy. You had red hair and looked just like your grandfather. Your father and I knew we would love you so much, and we knew nothing could ever take away our love for you. You used to talk to me with little baby sounds, and I would talk back to you even when I knew you didn't understand, just to tell you how special you were to me and how much I loved you.

> "Your eyes were so blue I almost never wanted you to sleep so I could keep looking at your beautiful eyes. Even when I got sick and had to go to the hospital right after you were born, I took you with me, because I never wanted to be away from you."

> When his mother tells him about his birth in such loving terms, Jordan becomes all ears. He listens so intently that he settles right down.

This is the kind of loving care your Heavenly Father has for you! In fact, the Bible says:

> *He will delight in you with gladness. With His love, He will calm all your fears. He will rejoice over you with joyful songs.* ZEPHANIAH 3:17B [NLT]

It's interesting to me that most of the epistles in the New Testament start and end with the phrase, *"grace and peace to you…"* If you let your Father's words of grace wash over you, you will find yourself secure and at peace.

Read these verses from Psalm 103 and allow yourself to be calmed by grace:

Why does grace have a calming effect?

How has your study of grace calmed you?

Pray through Psalm 103:1–12 today, thanking God for these truths!

O my soul, bless God. From head to toe, I'll bless his holy name!

O my soul, bless God,
    don't forget a single blessing!

He forgives your sins — every one.
    He heals your diseases — every one.
    He redeems you from hell — saves your life!
    He crowns you with love and mercy — a paradise crown.
    He wraps you in goodness — beauty eternal.
    He renews your youth — you're always young in his presence.

God makes everything come out right;
    he puts victims back on their feet.
He showed Moses how he went about his work,
    opened up his plans to all Israel.
God is sheer mercy and grace;
    not easily angered, he's rich in love.
He doesn't endlessly nag and scold,
    nor hold grudges forever.
He doesn't treat us as our sins deserve,
    nor pay us back in full for our wrongs.
As high as heaven is over the earth,
    so strong is his love to those who fear him.
And as far as sunrise is from sunset,
    he has separated us from our sins.

PSALM 103:1–12 (THE MESSAGE)

Simply Amazed By Grace

As I write this, I've just returned to my room at Mount Hermon Christian Conference Center. I was one of the speakers at a family camp all week and tonight was the final night. As is the tradition here, we ended by singing and sharing testimonies around the campfire and then it was time for communion.

The way they do communion here is this: People stand in a single-file line to receive the elements. Two ministers are at the front, one holding the plate of wafers, and the other the cup. Each person, in turn, is told by the first pastor, "The body of Christ, broken for you," and when that person takes the bread and dips it in the cup, the second minister tells them, "The blood of Christ, shed for you."

I was the first minister tonight, the one with the bread, so every single person in line got to me first. I looked at each one in turn and said, "The body of Christ, broken for you." I tried not to let it get impersonal so I attempted eye contact and if I saw a nametag I said their name: "Bill, this is the body of Christ, broken for *you*."

And what blew me away, because I wasn't expecting it, was the variety of reactions I saw. One by one they came, and one by one I watched.

*"The body of Christ, broken for **you**."*

Some seemed impatient, rushing through the ritual. Some actually looked bored. Some seemed to be barely holding back laughter — maybe nervous, maybe mocking, maybe giddy with joy.

"The body of Christ, broken for you."

Some had tears streaming down their faces. Some paused, closed their eyes, and whispered, "Thank you." I don't think they were thanking me. Others stared for a long time at the elements and seemed deep in thought before they partook.

*"The body of **Christ**, broken for **you**."*

As time went on, more people were crying, and I mean actually sobbing: the back-of-the-line people. Maybe that's because they had more time to think about it. But I think it had to do with the time it took them to get up and get in line. I think some of them were reluctant, maybe thinking they were unworthy, and then finally deciding in a deeply personal cathartic moment that they would receive communion after all. And perhaps thinking of a specific sin that they had been seeing as an obstacle just a moment before, now they remembered it was washed away, and they cried.

Here is my prayer for you: "I pray that you, being rooted and established in love, might have power, together with all the saints, to grasp how long and high and wide and deep is the love of Christ, and to know this love that surpasses knowledge — that you may be filled to the full measure of all the fullness of God!" (EPHESIANS 3:17–19)

As the line thinned I looked and saw an older disabled woman still seated in the last row, so the other pastor and I marched down the aisle to her with the elements and as she received them she was wide-eyed with gratitude. Then I saw a young man near her who had not come down the aisle and offered him communion but he firmly declined.

And I began to think, "I am having a God's eye view of communion right here."

He comes to each of us, the Lamb slain for us, one by one, and He sees not a mass of humanity but each face, each person, each soul, intimately. And just like at the cross — still 2,000 years later — some laugh, some weep, some look the other way.

So it is with grace, the word we use to describe the reason and the result of that sacrifice. You might think you've heard it all before. You might be bored, maybe impatient. But look at that old man in line behind you. You recognize him. The great intellectual, the Apostle of Grace, St. Paul.

Paul, who in his lifetime thought more about grace and taught more about grace than perhaps anyone else ever, yet he is sobbing and laughing as, at the end of eleven chapters of theology about grace in the book of Romans, he exclaims, *"Oh, the depth of the riches of the wisdom and knowledge of God!"* (ROMANS 11:33)

Paul, who after three chapters of theology about grace in Ephesians says, *"I pray that you… may… grasp how wide and long and high and deep is the love of Christ… that you may be filled to the full measure of all the fullness of God"* (EPHESIANS 3:17A, 18, 19B).

I hope you never feel like you have it all figured out. I hope you linger as you gaze at the price paid for you. Think of the love felt for you. Consider the sins washed from you. And become simply amazed by grace!

John Newton: The Rest of the Story

Through many dangers, toils and snares

I have already come;

We began this Grace Immersion with the story of John Newton's composition of the lyrics to "Amazing Grace," but that's just one highlight of a truly colorful life. Here's the rest of the story.

Newton was an only child beloved by his religiously devout mother. But when he was seven his mother died suddenly, leaving him in the care of his frequently absent seafaring father. He was allowed by his stepmother to run completely free, getting into all kinds of adolescent trouble.

Whenever he fell into temptation he'd feel horribly guilty, as if he was displeasing his dead mother. He'd vow to live up to her ideals. He'd turn to spiritual disciplines like rigorous prayer, reading religious literature only and studiously keeping spiritual diaries.

But at 17 he went on a months-long voyage as a sailor and soon took up smoking, swearing, and indulging every lust when in port. He'd still have pangs of guilt. Then on one of his ships he met the captain's clerk, a man named Mitchell. He was an atheist playboy who told Newton, "Life… was for the taking. God is a phantom invented by killjoy religious types. We must eat, drink, and be merry, for tomorrow we die and pass into extinction." (Quoted in an article by Chris Armstrong for *Christian History* magazine)

Newton was eager to escape the guilt and constraints of his mother's religion. After this he delighted in "deconverting" Christians, as he called it, just as he had been "deconverted" himself.

He soon became involved in the slave trade. Somehow his independent spirit annoyed his first employer so much that Newton himself was put in chains and made a servant. A few of the slaves had pity on him, snuck in food, and smuggled out a series of desperate letters addressed to his father.

Two years later a ship sent by his father rescued him, but Newton continued sailing in the slave trade, mistreating the very people who had helped him earlier, and reaching depths of immorality that shocked even the older sailors. One night he narrowly escaped death by drowning after he fell overboard during an alcohol-fueled party, but he had apparently *still* not hit bottom. That came when his ship went through the famous storm. The vessel began to split apart. One sailor was washed overboard. Tied to the ship to prevent being washed away, Newton steered the ship through the night. All the while he reviewed his life. Finally he prayed

How does the phrase "his kindness leads you to repentance" summarize what you've learned about grace?

What motivates you about the life of John Newton?

Today sing or think through the lyrics of "Amazing Grace" as a prayer, reviewing what God's done in your past and expecting great things, by His grace, in your future!

IF YOU'D LIKE TO CONTINUE YOUR GRACE IMMERSION, CHECK OUT THE BONUS MATERIAL INCLUDING 14 EXTRA DAILY MEDITATIONS AT www.GraceImmersion.com

that desperate prayer for God to save the ship and forgive him. As he was later to recall it, this was "the hour I first believed."

And so the prodigal returned home. He still found it embarrassing to talk about faith, he could not yet bring himself to pray with anyone, and he even sailed his slave ship for a while longer. But a small seed began to grow.

Newton left slave trading and became a customs inspector, eventually deciding to leave the shipping industry entirely to be a pastor. But the religious leaders of his day were less than enthused about the idea. By this time he'd started speaking about his conversion at "religious societies" and church authorities were suspicious of this maverick with a rough past. After completing his education as a pastor, Newton had to endure *seven years* of flat refusal from several bishops to ordain him! Finally one let him pastor a church in the tiny town of Olney, a place with only 2,000 people.

While there he was made famous by his best-selling autobiography, coming clean about everything in his past and focusing on God's amazing grace shown throughout his colorful life.

By 1800 no evangelical pastor in the world was more famous or more influential than John Newton. Yet Newton remained very humble, always aware of his past, calling himself "the old African blasphemer."

At 82, he said, "My memory is nearly gone, but I remember two things, that I am a great sinner, and that Christ is a great Saviour." I love that he focused on *Christ*, the grace-giver, not just grace as a *concept*. This is my hope for you.

As John Newton's tombstone reads,

> "John Newton, Clerk,
> once an infidel and libertine, a servant of slaves in Africa,
> was, by the rich mercy of our Lord and Saviour Jesus Christ,
> preserved, restored, pardoned, and appointed
> to preach the faith he had long labored to destroy."

'Tis Grace that brought me safe thus far
and Grace will lead me home.

SMALL GROUPS
Discussion Questions

Ocean-Sized Grace

Pray as you begin, asking God to be at work in your group. Introduce yourselves to one another.

Group Sharing

- Have each group member share an insight they gleaned from the daily meditations you read in the Grace Immersion book: Anything helpful, exciting, confusing, new?

- Was there anything about this last week's sermon that particularly touched you or grabbed you?

Video

Play the video for week 1. If your group doesn't have a DVD, you can watch or download each weekly video for free on the web at *www.GraceImmersion.com*

Meeting format

You may want to explain the format for these meetings:

1. Group Sharing

There is time allotted at the beginning of each weekly session for everyone to share any insights from their Grace Immersion daily readings. Come prepared to share an insight, a question, a favorite quote or verse, or anything else you'd like.

2. Video

Then the group watches the video clip introducing the weekly topic.

3. Response

Then it's time to respond to the topic and verses raised in the video, and to look up some more verses and hopefully gain more insight!

Questions with the key symbol 🔑 are essential for your small group meetings. We encourage you to answer as many questions as time allows, but don't miss the keys!

4. Prayer

Finally make sure you leave time for prayer requests and prayer at the end of each meeting.

Scriptures in the Video this Week

Are you so foolish? After beginning with the Spirit, are you now trying to attain your goal by human effort? GALATIANS 3:3

What has happened to all your joy? GALATIANS 4:15A

It is for freedom that Christ has set us free. Stand firm, then, and do not let yourselves be burdened again by a yoke of slavery! GALATIANS 5:1

You who are trying to be justified by law have been alienated from Christ; you have fallen away from grace. GALATIANS 5:4

"It is finished." JOHN 19:30

His divine power has given us everything we need for life and godliness through our knowledge of him who called us by his own glory and goodness. 2 PETER 1:3

Praise be to the God and Father of our Lord Jesus Christ, who has blessed us in the heavenly realms with every spiritual blessing in Christ. EPHESIANS 1:3

And you have been given fullness in Christ… COLOSSIANS 2:10A

And God is able to make all grace abound to you, so that in all things at all times, having all that you need, you will abound in every good work. 2 CORINTHIANS 9:8

He who did not spare his own Son, but gave him up for us all — how will he not also, along with him, graciously give us all things? ROMANS 8:32

Response

1. ⚷ Was there anything from the DVD that was new to you, or had an effect on you? Did you hear anything that raised more questions in your mind?

2. In what ways can you relate to René's story? Have some group members share their journey of understanding God's love and grace.

   a. In what ways have you sometimes tried to earn God's favor by your good works?

   b. Have you ever felt exhausted, cold, dry in your experience of God's favor? Describe your experience.

   c. Have you ever come to a fresh realization of God's grace poured out on your life? What happened?

📖 🔑 Have someone in your group read the following section out loud:

What is "Grace"?

The word "grace" is often misunderstood, even by Christians. In Greek it is used with far more meanings than can be represented by any one term in English. Sometimes we use it to mean "blessing" as in "saying grace," or a kind of elegance, as in "she moves with grace." But what does it mean in the Bible?

Our English word "grace" is a translation of the Greek word *charis* from which we get our word "charity." That root might help you see what it means in Greek: When the Bible speaks of God's grace it's not merely talking about an *attribute* of God (as in, God is "graceful", elegant, beautiful), although this is certainly part of the picture. But it means not *just* this; it also has to do with the *act* of *charitable giving*; lavishing gifts on those in need, who are unable to help themselves.

Here's the way one well-respected Greek scholar puts it:

In Paul … *charis* is never merely an attitude or disposition of God (God's character as gracious); consistently it denotes something much more dynamic — the wholly generous *act* of God… it denotes effective divine power in the experience of men. (James D.G. Dunn, *Romans 1–8*, p. 17)

The theologian Louis Berkhof echoes his thoughts:

Charis may denote *gracefulness* or *beauty*, but most generally means *favour* or *good-will*. The fundamental idea is that the blessings graciously bestowed are *freely* given, and not in consideration of any claim or merit. Furthermore, the word is expressive of the emotion awakened in the heart of the recipient of such favour, and thus acquires the meaning "gratitude" or "thankfulness." (Louis Berkhof, *Systematic Theology*, pp. 426–427)

"Grace" has also been defined as

- **G**od's **R**iches **A**t **C**hrist's **E**xpense

- God's unmerited favor

- Pardon freely given

An understanding of biblical grace can change everything about the way you perceive your religion, your motivations, God, others… in fact, life itself!

The chart on the following page may help you see how this happens.

PERFORMANCE-ORIENTED RELIGION	THE GOSPEL OF GRACE
"I obey, therefore I'm accepted"	"I'm accepted, therefore I obey"
Motivation: Fear and insecurity	Motivation: Security and grateful joy
Identity: Based on my performance; therefore criticism is devastating	Identity: Based on God's love for me therefore criticism may be a struggle but is taken much less personally
My prayer life is largely petition; I feel I must pray more, and pray better.	My prayer life is relaxed and has stretches of praise and adoration
Self-image: Swings between two extremes: I can feel proud and impatient with "lesser performers" when I'm doing well; then when I fall I feel like a miserable failure.	Self-image: I see myself as both sinful and yet also fully loved by God, lavished with his grace though I am undeserving.
My self-worth is based mainly on how hard I work or how moral I am — and I find myself looking down on the "lazy" or "immoral".	My self-image is centered on the One who died for me. I am saved by sheer grace so how could I look down on anyone?

(Chart adapted from *Gospel in Life: Grace Changes Everything* by Tim Keller)

3. Circle anything in the chart you feel is true of yourself. Is there anything you would like to change?

4. In your group, look at the devotion for Day 5. You may want to read it out loud. Can you relate to René … and Martha? How?

5. What are your expectations or hopes for this Grace Immersion?

6. How would you describe the big idea or main point from today's session?

Prayer

- Share group prayer requests (write them down on the pages available in the back of this book) and take time to pray.

- Before you go, make sure everyone fills out a sheet with names and contact information.

- Designate someone as your group "secretary", who can email everyone a reminder about next week's meeting.

- Decide what you'll do about munchies next week: Is someone providing a meal, or dessert?

- Remember that you can join the discussion on the Grace Immersion web site: *www.GraceImmersion.com*

Grace Robbers

Pray as you begin, asking God to be at work in your group.

Group Sharing

- Have each group member share a highlight and a "lowlight" from the week.

- Have each group member share an insight they gleaned from the daily meditations you read in the Grace Immersion book: Anything helpful, exciting, confusing, new?

- Was there anything about this last week's sermon that particularly touched you or grabbed you?

Video

Play the video for week 2. If your group doesn't have a DVD, you can watch or download each weekly video for free at *www.GraceImmersion.com*

Scriptures in the Video this Week

"Where is that sense of blessing you once had?"
GALATIANS 4:15 [NASB]

"So Christ has truly set us free. Now make sure that you stay free and don't get tied up again in slavery to the law." GALATIANS 5:1 [NLT]

They only want you to be circumcised so they can boast about it and claim you as disciples. GALATIANS 6:13B [NLT]

Questions to Diagnose Religious Addiction

1. Do you sense that God is looking at you and if you don't do enough He might turn on you, or not bless you?

2. Is it hard for you to make decisions? Even small ones?

3. Do you believe you are being punished for something you did in the past?

4. Do you feel if you work a little harder, God will finally forgive you?

5. Do you feel extreme guilt for being out of church just one Sunday, or missing just one day's Bible reading?

6. Do you have an obsessive focus on figuring out what's right and what's wrong?

(Condensed and abridged from from *Toxic Faith*, Steve Arterburn)

Response

1. 🔑 Was there anything from the DVD that was new to you, or had an effect on you? Did you hear anything that raised more questions in your mind?

2. 🔑 What is your response to Steve Arterburn's diagnostic questions on the previous page?

3. Have you ever been in a place where you were defining your spiritual health by the rules you follow?

   a. What's wrong with that approach? Aren't rules good?

   b. What if the rules were all out of the Bible? Do you think it would be a mistake to gauge my spirituality by how well I am keeping Biblical rules?

4. 🔑 If rules are not the biblical gauge for measuring spiritual health, then what is?

5. What is the goal of Christianity anyway, if not to produce rule-followers?

6. What's the matter with being obsessed with what's right and what's wrong?

📖 Read Galatians 5:16–25. Then have someone read this paragraph:

Paul doesn't really give a definitive list of prohibitions or rules in Galatians 5, but he does list actions that, while not a checklist of sins, are typical of someone living in what he calls "the flesh". And then, notice that he does not give a list of commands to keep; instead he gives a list of character qualities that are typical of someone walking in the Spirit.

7. 🔑 Why is Paul's method, listing character qualities, more effective than just giving lists of behaviors to do or to avoid?

8. Look back over the devotion from Day 9, particularly the closing paragraphs. In what area of your life are you lacking peace? How could an understanding of grace give you peace in that struggle?

9. How would you describe the big idea from today's session?

Your group may want to begin discussing a group Grace Project! There's a list of ideas on page 155.

Prayer

- Share group prayer requests (write them down on the pages available in the back of this book) and take time to pray.

- Decide what you'll do about munchies next week: Is someone providing a meal, or dessert?

- Remember that you can join the discussion on the Grace Immersion web site: *www.GraceImmersion.com*

No More Jail Time!

Pray as you begin, asking God to be at work in your group.

Group Sharing

- Have each group member share a highlight and a "lowlight" from the week.

- Have each group member share an insight they gleaned from the daily meditations you read in the Grace Immersion book: Anything helpful, exciting, confusing, new?

- Was there anything about this last week's sermon that particularly touched you or grabbed you?

Video

Play the video for week 3. If your group doesn't have a DVD, you can watch or download each weekly video for free at *www.GraceImmersion.com*.

Video Notes

"Therefore, there is now no condemnation for those who are in Christ Jesus…" ROMANS 8:1A

Two common responses when I sin:

1. Self-_____

However, *"No one will be declared righteous …by observing the law"* (ROMANS 3:20A).

2. Self-_____

An understanding of grace helps me realize that, because of Christ, I have escaped condemnation — so that I respond with gratitude through good works!

Response

1. 🔑 Was there anything from the DVD that was new to you, or had an effect on you? Did you hear anything that raised more questions in your mind?

2. 🔑 How do you deal with shame when you fall?

   • Self-justification: Convince yourself you're OK the way you are

   • Self-condemnation: Try to make up for our failure through shame and hard work

   • Some combination of the two (explain)

   • Receive God's grace

3. What does grace teach you about what to do when you fall?

4. How could the story of Thomas Doaks (the sailor who jumped ship and found refuge in a church — and then painted their altar as a gift) illustrate how grace works in our lives?

Let's explore the topic of guilt, condemnation, and forgiveness further through some Bible verses.

5. Who has sinned, according to Romans 3:23?

6. But hang in there! What does Romans 3:24 say about how we can be justified?

7. What is the penalty of sin, according to Romans 6:23?

8. But! Romans 6:23 goes on to say that though death should be our penalty, what is the gift of God?

9. Isn't it amazing: None of these verses tell us that our redemption or justification comes through working harder. It's a gift. Romans 5:8 tells us that, *"God demonstrated His love for us in that why we were still sinners Christ died for us."* It's a gift: Christ died for your sins, for your life. What do you have to do to receive this amazing grace gift, according to Romans 10:13?

📖 🔑 Maybe you have already called on the name of the Lord but you still struggle with feeling like you should be in "jail." Have someone in the group read Isaiah 61:1–3.

10. What do these verses tell you about God's grace? How can this encourage you when you feel like you deserve prison time?

📖 Turn to Colossians 2:13–14 and have someone read it out loud. Then have someone read this paragraph:

Imagine an invoice created by God for your sins. At the top it says, "To be paid for in eternity" and then it lists everything you have ever done wrong. Imagine some of the sins that could be on that list, an itemized record of everything you've ever done wrong. Then at the bottom it says, "Total: _____."

11. According to the Bible passage you just read, what is written in that blank by God?

    a. How does this help you with your shame?

📖 🔑 Please read Romans 7:21–8:3 and Hebrew 4:15–16.

12. How do you relate to Paul's description of his struggle with sin in the Romans passage?

After all Paul's talk about our struggle with sin in Romans chapter 7, you can understand why he'd say, "Thanks be to God…" when he turns the corner and starts talking about the grace we have through Jesus Christ. "Thanks be to God…" what refreshing words! "Thanks be to God…" that no matter what my sin, "There is no condemnation for those who are in Christ Jesus…" (ROMANS 8:1).

13. After thinking about the grace that God has poured on you, how do the verses in Hebrews 4:15–16 impact you?

14. 🔑 How would you describe the big idea from today's session?

15. Before you close, discuss and schedule your group Grace Project! There's a list of ideas on page 155.

Prayer

- Share group prayer requests (write them down on the pages available in the back of this book) and take time to pray.

- Decide what you'll do about munchies next week: Is someone providing a meal, or dessert?

- Remember that you can join the discussion on the Grace Immersion web site: *www.GraceImmersion. com*

If You Have Finished Your Grace Project, Debrief

1. How was it different than what you expected?

2. What sense of reward did you feel?

3. What insights did you gain, if any, about grace?

Grace Overflows

Pray as you begin, asking God to be at work in your group.

Group Sharing

- Have each group member share a highlight and a "lowlight" from the week.

- Have each group member share an insight they gleaned from the daily meditations you read in the Grace Immersion book: Anything helpful, exciting, confusing, new?

- Was there anything about this last week's sermon that particularly touched you or grabbed you?

Video

Play the video for week 4. If your group doesn't have a DVD, you can watch or download each weekly video for free at *www.GraceImmersion.com*

Video Notes

In this week's video we summarize and elaborate on points made in Timothy Keller's excellent resource, *Gospel In Life: Grace Changes Everything*.

What If People Don't Deserve Help?

Jesus said we are to *"do good"* even to the unrighteous… *"Then you will be sons of the Most High, because He is kind to the ungrateful and the wicked. Be merciful, as your Father is merciful."* (LUKE 6:35B–36) And Romans 12:20a says *"if your enemy is hungry, feed him…"*

> "A merely religious person, who believes God will favor him because of his morality and respectability, will ordinarily have contempt for the outcast. 'I worked hard to get where I am, and so can anyone else!' That is the language of the moralist's heart. A life poured out in deeds of mercy to the needy is the inevitable sign of someone who has grasped the doctrine of grace." – TIM KELLER

(continued on next page)

Why Should We as Christians Help Those in Need?

- Jesus said the church was to be a *"city on a hill"* (MATTHEW 5:14)

- Jesus said to *"do good"* to even your enemies (LUKE 6:33,35)

- Jesus taught the Samaritan's deeds of mercy (LUKE 10:33 says he was moved by compassion) were signs of godliness, as opposed to the busy religious lives of the priest and Levite

- Jesus tells us that when we feed the hungry or when we give the thirsty something to drink we are in essence also giving him food or drink (MATTHEW 25:40).

- Jesus, Isaiah, James, John, Paul, and many other Bible writers spoke of acts of mercy as a way to distinguish between true and false believers.

- In Acts 2:42–47 it says the early Christians even sold their possessions so they would have something to give to the poor.

- Job said, *"If I have denied the desires of the poor or let the eyes of the widow grow weary, if I have kept my bread to myself, not sharing it with the fatherless… then let my arm fall from the shoulder!"* (JOB 31:16–17,22A)

Motives Matter

Be cautious about your motive, though. Lots of books and preachers tell us to help the needy because we have so much. But as Keller says, this approach is very limited in its motivating power. "How selfish you are to eat steak and drive two cars when the rest of the world is starving!" This creates great emotional conflict in the heart of Christians… We feel guilty, but all sorts of defense mechanisms are engaged: "Can I help it if I was born in this country? Don't I have a right to enjoy the fruits of my labor?" Soon we just stop listening to people who make us feel guilty.

The Bible doesn't use guilt motivation. It uses grace motivation!

In 2 Corinthians 8, Paul tells the Corinthians how the Macedonian Christians gave so generously so the hungry victims of the Jerusalem famine could have food to eat. What does he say motivated them?

"Their overflowing joy…" 2 CORINTHIANS 8:2

"They gave themselves first to the Lord…" V. 5

"Mercy is spontaneous, superabounding love which comes from an experience of the grace of God. The deeper the experience of the free grace of God, the more generous we must become."
– TIM KELLER

Response

1.   Was there anything from the DVD that was new to you, or had an effect on you? Did you hear anything that raised more questions in your mind?

   Read Acts 2:42–47 (a passage that describes the early church) out loud in your group.

2. What do you learn about the early church from this passage?

    a. The early church was so involved with each other they had fellowship together "every day". In what way is that still possible today?

    b. What do you discover about the way the early church witnessed to others? How can you learn from this?

   Read the following comments from theologian Leslie Newbigin:

"The gospel does not become truth for a society by being propagated as a theory or a worldview and certainly not as a religion. It can become public truth only insofar as it is embodied in a society (the church) which is both 'abiding in' Christ and engaged in the life of the world." – LESLIE NEWBIGIN

3. How would you summarize his point? Do you agree? Why or why not?

   Read Isaiah 58:1–10.

4. What was the problem with the people's behavior (verses 3–6)?

5. What things does God say He would like to see His people doing?

6. Think about your motives for generosity. Are you generous because you are always remembering how generous God is with you? Or are you stingy — maybe because you see God that way?

7. The food bank is literally a bank of food — a silo, just like Joseph stored up in Egypt — saved for the poor so that we can be generous. What are some other ways you can be a bank of grace, ready to lavish blessings on people?

8. In what way does grace motivate you to do "good works"?

9. Why is it so important for works of mercy to be motivated by grace? What negative effects can a non-grace motivation have?

Read Luke 10:29–37.

10. The whole idea of helping your neighbor has always been surprisingly difficult to actually practice, then and now. Who is your neighbor? Make a short list of some people or groups that are in need around you.

11. How do people in your area typically view these groups? What emotions come to mind?

12. Discuss ways you and your group can show mercy to the poor, because you have been shown grace by God. Pray that you will find the time and the heart to volunteer. See the back of this book or go online to *www.GraceImmersion.com* for ideas!

13. How would you describe the big idea in today's session?

If You Have Finished Your Grace Project, Debrief

1. How was it different than what you expected?

2. What sense of reward did you feel?

3. What insights did you gain, if any, about grace?

Prayer

- Share group prayer requests (write them down on the pages available in the back of this book) and take time to pray.

- Decide what you'll do about munchies next week: Is someone providing a meal, or dessert?

- Remember that you can join the discussion on the Grace Immersion web site: *www.GraceImmersion.com*

Grace-Motivated Holiness

Pray as you begin, asking God to be at work in your group.

Group Sharing

- Have each group member share a highlight and a "lowlight" from the week.

- Have each group member share an insight they gleaned from the daily meditations you read in the Grace Immersion book: Anything helpful, exciting, confusing, new?

- Was there anything about this last week's sermon that particularly touched you or grabbed you?

Video

Play the video for week 5. If your group doesn't have a DVD, you can watch or download each weekly video for free at *www.GraceImmersion.com*

Scriptures in the Video This Week

You, my brothers, were called to be free. But do not use your freedom to indulge the sinful nature; rather, serve one another in love. GALATIANS 5:13

Godless men… change the grace of our God into a license for immorality. JUDE 1:4A

You are free… but don't use your freedom as an excuse to do evil. 1 PETER 2:16 [NLT]

…you are a slave of whatever controls you. 2 PETER 2:19B [NLT]

Response

1. Was there anything from the DVD that was new to you, or had an effect on you? Did you hear anything that raised more questions in your mind?

2. 🔑 In what ways are Christians today tempted to "eat the garbage"? How about you? Why do we eat the garbage instead of the barbecued food?

📖 🔑 Read 1 John 3:1–6.

3. I love this passage! True, it's a call to be pure, to live a life that reflects our faith in God. But where does John start this call to purity? Does he start it by berating us? No! He begins by telling us who we are because of who God is. According to 1 John 3:1 what are God's feelings towards you and what is your position in His "family"?

   a. *"How great the love the Father has lavished on us…"* For years I read this verse and felt no emotion except guilt. I'd think, "God lavishes love and yet I'm so stupid!" and so I just hardened my heart to feel nothing but intellectual assent. I cannot describe the emotional "dam" that broke when I realized that God had already lavished His love on me. It's a done deal. I'm loved because of Him not because of me! How I interpret the rest of the passage hinges on trusting God's lavish love first.

   b. In what way have you struggled with trusting God's lavish love for you?

4. Think about your closest relationships. How does love impact your motivation and actions in those relationships?

5. How would you like to see God's love impact your motivation and actions in your relationship with Him?

6. 🔑 Look back over the devotion from Day 21. Describe a "Grand Canyon" moment you've had.

7. Have you ever been "propelled by awe" for God? In what area of your life could awe for God impact your motivation to obey away from drudgery and closer to gratitude?

8. ⊶ How would you describe the big idea of today's session?

Prayer

- Share group prayer requests (write them down on the pages available in the back of this book) and take time to pray.

- Decide what you'll do about munchies next week: Is someone providing a meal, or dessert?

- Remember that you can join the discussion on the Grace Immersion web site: *www.GraceImmersion. com*

If You Have Finished Your Grace Project, Debrief

1. How was it different than what you expected?

2. What sense of reward did you feel?

3. What insights did you gain, if any, about grace?

Radical Grace

Pray as you begin, asking God to be at work in your group.

Group Sharing

- Have each group member share a highlight and a "lowlight" from the week.

- Have each group member share an insight they gleaned from the daily meditations you read in the Grace Immersion book: Anything helpful, exciting, confusing, new?

- Was there anything about this last week's sermon that particularly touched you or grabbed you?

Video

Play the video for week 6. If your group doesn't have a DVD, you can watch or download each weekly video for free at *www.GraceImmersion.com*

Video Notes

Response

1. 🔑 What do you think about what you just saw?

2. Do you think you could do something like that?

3. 🔑 Do you think that's really asked of us, to forgive like that? Why or why not? What do you think is the key to Lynn's ability to forgive? How is understanding grace a part of this?

4. What about someone in a dangerous situation: someone is beating them up at school or at home. Are they to just forgive and keep getting beaten up?

5. 🔑 What is the difference between forgiveness and trust?

📖 🔑 Have someone in your group read the following passages out loud:

Live in harmony with one another… Do not repay evil for evil… if it is possible, as far as it depends on you, live at peace with everyone. Do not take revenge, my friends, but leave room for God's wrath, for it is written: "It is mine to avenge; I will repay," says the Lord. On the contrary, "If your enemy is hungry, feed him. If he is thirsty, give him something to drink. In doing this you will heap burning coals on his head." Do not be overcome with evil, but overcome evil with good. ROMANS 12:16–20

Be kind and compassionate to one another, forgiving each other, just as in Christ God forgave you. EPHESIANS 4:32

See to it that no one misses the grace of God and that no bitter root grows up to cause trouble and defile many. HEBREWS 12:15

6. How does an awareness of how Christ forgave you lead to kindness, compassion, and forgiveness toward others?

7. How does missing the grace of God lead to "bitter" roots?

8. Read the daily meditation from Day 33. Graciousness is a result of "being graced" by God. One aspect is forgiveness. Other facets of a gracious spirit:

- Listening well

- Using kind words

- Smiling

- Giving others the benefit of the doubt

- Gentleness

- Write down some other aspects of a gracious spirit here:

    a. Which facets of graciousness are you best at? In which facet do you need to grow the most?

    b. Let's talk about some of these aspects of gracious living: How, for example, can you grow better at listening well? When do you struggle most with being a gracious listener?

9.   Practice "grace" with one another in your group. Since graciousness is part of our response to grace, exercise kindness, encouragement, gentleness, and love right now! Go around the room having all your group members affirm each person in turn. Mention a character quality or action that you have noticed.

10.   Jesus made it clear that if we have truly received grace, we will want to give grace. Think about ways you will put your faith into action, showing grace in practical ways this week. Share some ideas with your group.

11. How would you describe the big idea from this week's session?

Before you close, discuss and schedule your group Grace Project if you haven't yet. There's a list of ideas on page 155.

Prayer

- Share group prayer requests (write them down on the pages available in the back of this book) and take time to pray.

- Decide what you'll do about munchies next week: Is someone providing a meal, or dessert?

- Remember that you can join the discussion on the Grace Immersion web site: *www.GraceImmersion. com*

If You Have Finished Your Grace Project, Debrief

1. How was it different than what you expected?

2. What sense of reward did you feel?

3. What insights did you gain, if any, about grace?

Drenched in Grace

Pray as you begin, asking God to be at work in your group.

Group sharing

- Have each group member share a highlight and a "lowlight" from the week.

- Have each group member share an insight they gleaned from the daily meditations you read in the Grace Immersion book: Anything helpful, exciting, confusing, new?

- Was there anything about this last week's sermon that particularly touched you or grabbed you?

Video

Play the video for week 7. If your group doesn't have a DVD, you can watch or download each weekly video for free at *www.GraceImmersion.com*

Scriptures in the Video This Week

I give waters in the wilderness and rivers in the desert, to give drink to my people... ISAIAH 43:20 [NASB]

The poor and needy search for water, but there is none; their tongues are parched with thirst. But I the LORD will answer them; I, the God of Israel, will not forsake them. I will make rivers flow on barren heights, and springs within the valleys. I will turn the desert into pools of water, and the parched ground into springs. ISAIAH 41:17–18

Whoever drinks the water I give him will never thirst. Indeed, the water I give him will become in him a spring of water welling up to eternal life. JOHN 4:14

Response

1. 🔑 Was there anything from the DVD that was new to you, or had an effect on you? Did you hear anything that raised more questions in your mind?

2. If grace is real, why does our image and our experience of the Christian life not always reflect this?

3. 🔑 If God showers His blessings on me, why do I not always notice or feel it?

4. What can I do to make sure this is more typical of my Christian experience — reveling in the living water poured out on me?

5. If God showers his blessings on us, why are we so often so stingy in what we give — and forgive? Where does that stinginess come from if it doesn't come from God?

6. 🔑 In what ways have you — or your perception of your faith — changed as a result of this grace immersion?

📖 Read Ephesians 3:14–21.

7. This is the classic prayer of Paul for the church in Ephesus. Something I find fascinating about this prayer is that not once does Paul pray for the Ephesians to work harder at sharing their faith, or send him more money for his ministry. Make a list of what Paul does pray for the Ephesians:

Now, take a moment to fill in your name in Paul's prayer and then read the prayer over to yourself twice.

For this reason I kneel before the Father, from whom his whole family in heaven and on earth derives its name. I pray that out of his glorious riches he may strengthen _____ with power through his Spirit in _____'s inner being, so that Christ may dwell in _____'s heart through faith. And I pray that _____, being rooted and established in love, may have power, together with all the saints, to grasp how wide and long and high and deep is the love of Christ, and to know this love that surpasses knowledge—that _____ may be filled to the measure of all the fullness of God.

Now to him who is able to do immeasurably more than all we ask or imagine, according to his power that is at work within us, to him be glory in the church and in Christ Jesus throughout all generations, for ever and ever! Amen. EPHESIANS 3:14–21

8. Now share with the group how you see God's grace towards you in this prayer. How does this prayer encourage you today?

9. 🔑 How would you describe the key idea from this lesson and the whole series?

Prayer

- Share group prayer requests (write them down on the pages available in the back of this book) and take time to pray.

- Decide what you'll do about continuing with another study, or taking a break.

- Remember that you can join the discussion on the Grace Immersion web site: *www.GraceImmersion.com*

RESOURCES
Project Ideas, Music Playlist & Print Materials

Grace Project Ideas

But just as you excel in everything — in faith, in speech, in knowledge, in complete earnestness and in your love for us — see that you also excel in this grace of giving. 2 Corinthians 8:7

Paul tells us to "excel" in the grace of giving — that is, to exercise that muscle regularly. What are some ways you can do this through grace projects?

Food Drives
Raise money or food at your church for the hungry people in your community or in an area of famine (this was the original grace project suggested by Paul in 2 Corinthians 8).

Garage Sales (or eBay Sales!)
Sell some of your stuff and give all the proceeds to those in need (This was a grace project done by the church in Acts 2:45). You could donate to the Salvation Army, your church, a local food pantry, or a missionary you know.

Help a Neighbor
Go to the home of an elderly or disabled person and offer to mow their lawn or wash their car — for free, of course, or it wouldn't be grace!

Face-to-Face Grace
Volunteer to serve with an inner-city church or a rescue mission. Try to help out in ways that involve direct, face-to-face contact with the people in need — for example, a group from our church recently served with a ministry in San Francisco and literally washed the feet of homeless people there (One note: Be sure to receive guidance from the people already leading these ministries instead of blindly charging into dangerous or culturally volatile areas with your own ideas).

Volunteer Grace

Go to a local charity that helps people in need but is strapped for cash — for example, a homeless services center or a disabled children's center. Offer to volunteer with your family or small group for an entire day, doing whatever they need.

Showing Grace to Your City or Schools

Call up a local school or city. These days, every school district and municipality seems to be strapped for cash. Tell them your family, small group, or church would like to help out one Saturday doing whatever is needed — no strings attached.

Grace at Home

How can you "excel in the grace of giving" at your own house? Look around. Are there projects that need to be done? Are there daily chores with which you can help? If you need direction, ask your family members.

Grace at Church

And finally consider how you can "exercise the grace of giving" at your own church. Is your giving so comfortable that you don't even notice it anymore, even though it was a stretch at first? Maybe it's time to stretch yourself again. What about serving in an area of ministry? If your church is like most, it needs you!

Grace Playlist

Download some songs about grace (legally of course!), and then listen to them as you drive around or at work or at play as part of this immersive experience! Here are some of my favorites. Add your own ideas on our web site: *www.GraceImmersion.com*

Note: I enjoy an extremely broad range of musical styles, so these may not all be to your taste. But download a few, make them your daily soundtrack, and let the power of music be part of your Grace Immersion!

Hymns, hymn-like songs and standards
Amazing Grace

Grace Greater Than All Our Sin

Wonderful Grace of Jesus

In Christ Alone *Keith and Kristen Getty*

How Deep The Father's Love For Us *Keith and Kristen Getty*

The Power of the Cross *Keith and Kristen Getty*

People Get Ready *(One good version is the live one by Seal)*

Grace (Lord I'm Grateful) *Stuart Townend*

Newer songs
By Your Side *Tenth Avenue North*

Amazing Grace (My Chains Are Gone) *Chris Tomlin*

Grace Like Rain *Todd Agnew*

Only Grace *Matthew West*

Grace *Laura Story*

Born Again *Third Day*

From The Inside Out *Seventh Day Slumber*

Alive *Pocket Full of Rocks*

Grace *Phil Wickham*

Except For Grace *The Martins*

Amazed *Lincoln Brewster*

Marvelous Light *Charlie Hall*

Healing Grace *Rick Muchow*

Forgiven *Sanctus Real*

Healing Begins *Tenth Avenue North*

The Love of God *Lincoln Brewster*

Lay 'Em Down *Needtobreathe*

Born Again *Newsboys*

By Your Side *Tenth Avenue North*

> Why are you striving these days
> Why are you trying to earn grace

Grace *Laura Story*

> I ask you: "How many times will you pick me up,
> when I keep on letting you down?
> And each time I will fall short of Your glory,
> how far will forgiveness abound?"
> And you answer: "My child, I love you.
> And as long as you're seeking My face,
> You'll walk in the pow'r of My daily sufficient grace."
> You are so patient with me, Lord.

People Get Ready

> You don't need no ticket,
> You just get on board

Grace Resources

I immersed myself in a study of grace while researching and writing this "Grace Immersion" book and enjoyed every minute of it. You'll notice I quoted liberally from several authors whose books I found thought-provoking and inspiring. If you're interested in reading more, I hope you'll enjoy exploring some of their volumes on this list. I don't necessarily agree with every word written in every single one of these books, but I found them all to have points that helped me appreciate new facets of the jewel of grace!

Amazing Grace *James Montgomery Boice*

Whatever Happened to the Gospel of Grace *James Mongomery Boice*

The Disciplines of Grace: God's Role and Our Role in the Pursuit of Holiness *Jerry Bridges*

Transforming Grace: Living Confidently in God's Unfailing Love *Jerry Bridges*

Transforming Grace: Living Confidently in God's Unfailing Love (Discussion Guide) *Jerry Bridges*

Holiness By Grace: Delighting in the Joy that is our Strength *Bryan Chapell*

In the Grip of Grace: When You Can't Hang On *Bryan Chapell*

You Can Change *Tim Chester*

The Performance Illusion *Chap Clark*

The Pressure's Off *Larry Crabb*

Heaven *W.A. Criswell & Paige Patterson*

The Liberty of Obedience *Elisabeth Elliot*

Growing in Grace *Bob George*

Grace Plus Nothing *Jeff Harkin*

Becoming A Woman of Grace *Cynthia Heald*

The Subtle Power of Spiritual Abuse *David Johnson & Jeff VanVonderen*

Gospel in Life: Grace Changes Everything *Timothy Keller*

Gospel in Life: Grace Changes Everything (DVD series) *Timothy Keller*

The God of the Second Chance: Experiencing Forgiveness *Greg Laurie*

In the Grip of Grace *Max Lucado*

Our Sufficiency in Christ *John MacArthur Jr.*

The Grace Walk *Steve McVey*

The Grace Walk Experience *Steve McVey*

The God Who Won't Let Go *Dean Merrill*

For the Audience of One *Mike Pilavachi*

Healing Grace *David A. Seamands*

Shame and Grace: Healing the Shame We Don't Deserve *Lewis B. Smedes*

Why Grace Changes Everything *Chuck Smith*

The Reign of Grace: The Delights and Demands of God's Love *Scotty Smith*

The Grace Awakening *Charles Swindoll*

Free Book *Brian Tome*

Surprised by Grace: God's Relentless Pursuit of Rebels *Tullian Tchividjian*

Uncommon Graces: Christlike Respones to a Hostile World *John Vawter*

Tired of Trying to Measure Up *Jeff VanVonderen*

What's So Amazing About Grace? *Philip Yancey*

Grace Verses

Here are some verses about grace that have become favorites of mine during this study. I encourage you to immerse yourself in them, memorize them, enjoy them!

From the fullness of his grace we have all received one blessing after another. JOHN 1:16

For all have sinned and fall short of the glory of God, and are justified freely by his grace through the redemption that came by Christ Jesus. ROMANS 3:23–24

It is for freedom that Christ has set us free. Stand firm, then, and do not let yourselves be burdened again by a yoke of slavery. GALATIANS 5:1

In him we have redemption through his blood, the forgiveness of sins, in accordance with the riches of God's grace that he lavished on us with all wisdom and understanding. EPHESIANS 1:7–8

But because of his great love for us, God, who is rich in mercy, made us alive with Christ even when we were dead in transgressions—it is by grace you have been saved. EPHESIANS 2:4–5

For it is by grace you have been saved, through faith—and this not from yourselves, it is the gift of God—not by works, so that no one can boast. For we are God's workmanship, created in Christ Jesus to do good works, which God prepared in advance for us to do. EPHESIANS 2:8–10

Let your conversation be always full of grace, seasoned with salt, so that you may know how to answer everyone. COLOSSIANS 4:6

Let us then approach the throne of grace with confidence, so that we may receive mercy and find grace to help us in our time of need. HEBREWS 4:16

See to it that no one misses the grace of God and that no bitter root grows up to cause trouble and defile many. HEBREWS 12:15

Do not be carried away by all kinds of strange teachings. It is good for our hearts to be strengthened by grace, not by ceremonial foods, which are of no value to those who eat them. HEBREWS 13:9

Therefore, prepare your minds for action; be self-controlled; set your hope fully on the grace to be given you when Jesus Christ is revealed. 1 PETER 1:13

But I am afraid that just as Eve was deceived by the serpent's cunning, your minds may somehow be led astray from your sincere and pure devotion to Christ. 2 CORINTHIANS 11:3

And God is able to make all grace abound to you, so that in all things at all times, having all that you need, you will abound in every good work. 2 CORINTHIANS 9:8

Prayer Requests

Request	Name	Date

Prayer Requests

Request   Name   Date

Prayer Requests

Request   Name   Date

Prayer Requests

Request   Name   Date

_____

_____

_____

_____

_____

_____

_____

_____

_____

_____

_____

_____

_____

_____

_____

_____

_____

_____

_____

_____

Prayer Requests

Request   Name   Date
_____

_____

_____

_____

_____

_____

_____

_____

_____

_____

_____

_____

_____

_____

_____

_____

_____

_____

_____

Thank You!

There were so many great people who offered helpful suggestions and advice that I simply cannot thank them all. But I'd like to express my deepest gratitude to seven people specifically without whom this *Grace Immersion* may not ever have been produced: Kevin Deutsch for his masterful layout work, Kelly Welty for his artistic production of the small group videos, Noel Smith and Mark Spurlock for their insightful editorial suggestions, Kevin Plaskett for his file preparation, Heidi Heath Garwood for her contribution to the cover art, and of course Valerie Webb for her essential shepherding of this whole process. And to the congregation of Twin Lakes Church: You are a wonderful source of support and friendship, just as Jesus intended a church to be!